AS Mu Revision

Richard Knight

www.rhinegoldeducation.co.uk

Music Study Guides
GCSE, AS and A2 Music Study Guides (AQA, Edexcel and OCR)
GCSE, AS and A2 Music Listening Tests (AQA, Edexcel and OCR)
GCSE, AS and A2 Music Revision Guides (AQA, Edexcel and OCR)
AS/A2 Music Technology Study Guide, Listening Tests, AS and A2 Revision Guides (Edexcel)

Also available from Rhinegold Education
AS and A2 Music Harmony Workbooks
GCSE and AS Music Composition Workbooks
GCSE and AS Music Literacy Workbooks
Romanticism in Focus, Baroque Music in Focus,
Modernism in Focus, Musicals in Focus , Film Music in Focus
Music Technology from Scratch
Understanding Popular Music
Careers in Music

First published 2014 in Great Britain by
Rhinegold Education
14–15 Berners Street
London W1T 3LJ, UK

www.rhinegoldeducation.co.uk

© Rhinegold Education 2014
a division of Music Sales Limited

You should always check the current requirements of the examination, as these may change.
Copies of the AQA specification can be downloaded from the AQA website at www.aqa.org.uk
AQA Publications (queries only) telephone 0844 209 6614, fax 0161 836 4545,
email: publications@aqa.org.uk

AQA AS Music Revision Guide 2nd edition
Order No. RHG109
ISBN: 978-1-78305-580-7

Exclusive Distributors:
Music Sales Ltd
Distribution Centre, Newmarket Road
Bury St Edmunds, Suffolk IP33 3YB, UK

Printed in the EU

Contents

The author

Richard Knight read music at St. John's College, Oxford, and has been Director of Music at two leading independent schools. He now combines teaching with a position as a senior examiner with one of the A level boards and is also on the examiner panel for the ABRSM. He has written several books for Rhinegold Education including study guides for GCSE, AS and A2 levels. Richard is also a composer with a diverse range of works to his name, including opera, oratorio and chamber music.

Acknowledgements

The author would like to thank the Rhinegold editorial and design team for their expert support in the preparation of this book.

Copyright

Companion website and audio

Throughout the book you will see the following icon:

This icon means there is audio available on the book's companion website to accompany the exercise. Go to www.rhinegoldeducation.co.uk, register, go to My Account and enter the code EK193 which will unlock the content to support this book. The numbers in the icons relate to the track numbers on the website.

You'll also find scores here to help you with the specimen questions.

Some of the exercises require you to access a piece of music. Rhinegold Education have created a YouTube playlist of the recommended clips. You'll see a YouTube icon next to these exercises, with clip number to help you find it in the playlist. Links to the videos are available on the website, or access the playlist here:

http://tinyurl.com/7scb28g

Introduction and about the exam

In order to gain your AS in music with AQA, you will need to complete the following sections:

- Unit 1: Influences on Music (worth 30% of total AS marks)
- Unit 2: Composing: Creating Musical Ideas (worth 30% of total AS marks)
- Unit 3: Performing: Interpreting Musical Ideas (worth 40% of total AS marks).

The focus of this revision guide will primarily be on Unit 1. In particular, you will find:

- Material to help you prepare for the listening questions in Section A
- Analytical information on the set work in a special revision format for Section B
- Revision notes on music relevant to each of the various options in Section C
- Advice on how to write good essays for questions you will answer in Sections B and C.

Also in this book you will find advice on making final preparations for submitting your composition in Unit 2.

Finally, there is some help for candidates approaching their Unit 3 performance.

Remember: your final result does not only reflect how musical, intelligent and enthusiastic you are; a large factor is how well you have done what the examiners want you to do. There are no marks available for the fantastic performance you gave in a concert at Christmas, or how many books about your set work you have read, or how many hours of listening to the music in your chosen Area of Study 2 you have put in over the past 6 months. The examiners can only give marks for how well you have done the tasks required of you in the specification, and they can only do this according to their published mark schemes.

This book is intended to help you to access as many of those marks as your other skills allow, and not trip up over the business of taking the exam.

Good luck!

Top ten tips

1. PLAN YOUR USE OF TIME

Units 2 and 3 have the same deadline for submitting your work: 15 May. Your Unit 1 exam could be as little as a week after this. You will also have other subjects to think about at this very intense time. You do not want to leave all your revision to the last moment.

2. REGULARLY TRAIN YOUR EAR

Half of the marks on the Unit 1 paper are available in Section A: the listening questions. It is very unlikely you will do well if you leave preparing for this to the last minute: the relevant parts of your body (your ears and brain) need training. A sprinter would spend many weeks getting into shape before an important 100m race; you need to be listening to, and thinking about, music every day over a long period of time before you sit this exam. Remember that listening is not the same as hearing. Having music on in the background while you are thinking about something else is hearing; listening means you are concentrating solely on the sounds reaching your ears.

3. LISTEN TO A WIDE RANGE OF MUSIC

The examiners have a huge range of music that they can draw on for Section A questions. In the 2012–2014 papers there were questions based on music by Bach, Haydn, Mozart, Beethoven, Schubert, Borodin, Saint-Saëns, Ravel, Vaughan Williams, Stravinsky, Orff, Milhaud and Copland. The more you listen to (not just hear) music across a similarly wide range of styles, the less chance there is that you could be caught out in the exam by something unfamiliar to you.

4. LISTEN REGULARLY TO YOUR SET WORK

You will be doing lots of analytical study of your set work, which is important, but – ultimately – music is an aural experience and you should be making yourself fully familiar with the musical experience of listening to the two movements of Haydn's 104th symphony. Listening to it should help to cement in place your understanding of the analytical detail you have studied, for you will associate theory with the sound and musical effect.

5. USE YOUR INSTRUMENTAL SKILLS TO PLAY YOUR SET WORK

Whatever instrument you play, you can engage with Haydn's symphony practically. If you are very fortunate you will play in an orchestra that can read through the two movements during a rehearsal; but even if this experience is not available to you, you can play or sing some part of it somehow. Pianists might like to explore the various arrangements available at http://imslp.org, which include versions for piano solo, piano duet and even eight hands at two pianos; there is also an arrangement for flute, two violins, viola and cello. Other instrumentalists or singers can play (or sing) along to the recording, following an appropriate line. Even percussionists can gain from playing the rhythms of the important themes as they come along. The combination of reading the notation with the concentration required to play the music whilst hearing the resulting sounds is a tremendous boost to your brain that has to cope with the challenge of assimilating all the information about this piece.

6. READ YOUR SCORE IN SILENCE, JUST LIKE A BOOK

As you sit reading this revision guide it is not necessary for you to be reading it aloud: the words make sense to your eyes, and – should you wish – you can imagine the sound of someone saying the words out loud as you read. The same should be true for your reading of the musical score. If you have listened (not heard) to the symphony played often enough, you should be able to read the musical score and imagine inside your head the sound of the music being played. This is a huge advantage when you are sat in silence in the exam room writing an essay about the music. Let your eyes follow the score at the tempo of the music, and enjoy your own personal performance inside your mind!

7. ORGANISE YOUR ANALYTICAL INFORMATION INTO CATEGORIES

There is a big danger in Section B that you will include in your essay lots of good information that is not relevant to the question that the examiners have asked. Be methodical: you need to be able to cover each section of the two movements: the introduction, exposition, development, recapitulation and coda. You also need to be able to focus on whichever aspect(s) the question demands: melody, rhythm, harmony and tonality, texture, instrumentation and structure. Organise your revision notes accordingly.

8. WHICHEVER AREA OF STUDY 2 YOU HAVE DONE, APPLY TIPS 5–7 AND LEARN SOME RELEVANT MUSICAL QUOTES

There is absolutely no point spending time writing out quotes in Section B: the examiners know you have a score in the exam room, so just refer to bar numbers. However, in Section C, providing pertinent musical quotes on the manuscript paper that is provided makes a good impression. It is also a much more musical skill than learning bar numbers!

9. MAKE SURE YOUR WRITTEN SUBMISSION FOR UNIT 2 SHOWS YOU HAVE TAKEN CARE

The composing unit does not just rely on how your work sounds: the quality of the written score or annotation makes a big impression on the examiner. It is usually more important than the recording. If you are doing Brief A, check thoroughly for errors such as parallel 5ths or missing 3rds, and make sure that your score for question 2 is well edited with tempo and performance markings. If you are doing Brief B or C, make sure your musical intentions are clear, that you have communicated the musical character of your work and that the material you are providing allows the examiner to follow the recording with the most helpful score or annotation that you can provide.

10. MAKE SURE YOUR RECORDING FOR UNIT 3 IS AS PRECISE AS POSSIBLE

No matter how vibrant the atmosphere in the room when you perform, or (for those taking the alternative options) how advanced your IT is, the moderator will only have the audio recording to assess your work. Make sure it does you justice!

Unit 1 – an overview

Content

Unit 1 is tested through a written examination. This lasts for 1 hour and 45 minutes and comes in **three** sections:

SECTION A: LISTENING

Four questions based on excerpts of unprepared music with short-answer questions, the answers for which are available through careful listening to the music, drawing on your general musical knowledge.

SECTION B: AREA OF STUDY 1

Two essay questions on the compulsory Haydn London Symphony set work will be on the exam paper; you only have to answer **one**.

SECTION C: AREA OF STUDY 2

For each of the three options for this Area of Study there will be two essay questions (making six in all): you only have to answer **one**.

Taking the exam

Your exam will start with the listening section. This involves extracts of music being played out loud in the exam room. The invigilators will have a CD and, as the exam starts, one of the invigilators will press 'play'.

The next half-hour (approximately) of the exam is governed by the CD. After the initial announcement on the CD there will be a silence of 3 minutes in which you can read the question paper. In this time:

- You **should** read the questions for Section A carefully. You may like to highlight any key words in the questions to help you focus your listening on the important points.
- You **could** look ahead to the essay questions for Sections B and C. You might be able to select the title for one of the essays you will be writing and spend some of this time jotting down some sense of an essay plan.
- **Do not** go into a trance and just wait for the next instruction from the voice on the CD.

The music for each question will be played two, three or four times. This will be stated on the question paper and announced on the CD at the start of each question.

When the final playing for the music of the final question in Section A has finished, there will be approximately 1 hour 15 minutes of the exam left for you to write your two essays (one in Section B, the other in Section C). You therefore need to be prepared to write your best essay answers in about 35 minutes per question.

Make sure you keep an eye on the time, and do not spend an hour on the first essay.

You may answer Section C first, should you wish.

Unit 1 – Section A: Listening

The listening section tests both your aural perception and your technical knowledge of musical language. AQA provide a list of terms that you should know and be able to recognise; this can be found on page 5 of the specification. Some of these terms are unlikely to occur in the listening questions (for instance, the terms listed under 'form': these are very difficult to incorporate into aural perception tests); in addition, some other rudimentary terms may be needed in the exam.

NOTE

Your teacher may have a hard copy of the specification you can use; alternatively, it is easy to find online at www.aqa.org.uk.

Definitions for these terms can be found in the Glossary on page 94 of this book. To help you revise, here are a series of exercises for each category (rhythm, melody, harmony, etc.). These are followed by some specimen questions on page 19 that you can do using recordings available online (see Note at the bottom of this page).

NOTE

The exercises are not necessarily AS-style questions, but are designed to improve the focus of your listening and sharpen your understanding of terminology. The specimen questions from page 19 onwards are in more of an AS style.

Exercises

RHYTHM

Rhythm is the fundamental aspect of most styles of music. We often 'feel' it, but we need to apply conscious thought to it in order to 'listen' to it. The following exercises are designed to help you recognise the following terms:

augmentation, diminution, additive rhythm, dotted rhythm, triplet, syncopation, hemiola, accelerando, ritenuto.

NOTE

Go to www.rhinegoldeducation.co.uk, register, go to My Account and enter the code EK193, which will unlock the supplementary resources for this book. All the audio for these exercises indicated with the following icon are given there.

The answers and comments to the exercises can be found from pages 62–79.

🔊 1 EXERCISE 1

Listen to the rhythm being played in Track 1. Then answer the following questions:

a. What metre (or time signature) is the rhythm in?
b. How many bars long is the rhythm?
c. Identify two bars that have an identical rhythm to each other.
d. What is the relationship between bars 1–2 and bar 3?
e. What rhythmic device is used in bar 4?
f. Which technique affects the rhythm towards the end?

🔊 2 EXERCISE 2

Listen to the rhythm being played in Track 2. Then answer the following questions:

a. What metre (or time signature) is the rhythm in?
b. How many bars long is the rhythm?
c. On which beat of the bar does the rhythm start?
d. What type of rhythmic figure is used in bar 3?
e. What type of rhythmic figure is used at the start of the second half of bars 5 and 6?
f. What rhythmic device is used in bars 7 and 8?

🔊 3 EXERCISE 3

Listen to the rhythm being played in Track 3. Then answer the following questions:

a. What metre (or time signature) is the rhythm in?
b. How many beats are there in each bar?
c. How many notes occur before the first barline?
d. What note value is the first note?
e. Which bar has the fewest notes in it?
f. What technique affects the rhythm towards the end?

🔊 4 EXERCISE 4

Listen to the rhythm being played in Track 4. Then answer the following questions:

a. What kind of metre is being used here to give a lively feel?
b. How many beats are there in each bar?
c. What is unusual about the fourth beat of each bar?
d. How many bars in total are there?
e. How do bars 5 and 6 differ from bars 1 and 2?

MELODY

Melody is often the most obvious aspect of music to listen to, as it is usually at the top of the texture and tends to be the part of a piece that we remember best after the music is played.

The next set of exercises are designed to help you recognise the following terms:

> conjunct, disjunct, triadic, blue notes, diatonic, scalic, pentatonic, whole tone, sequence, inversion, glissando.

The exercises also should help you to recognise melodic intervals and various ornaments.

◀)) 5 EXERCISE 5

Listen to the melody being played in Track 5. Then answer the following questions:

a. Is the melody in a major or minor key?
b. Which two words best describe the contour of the opening four bars of the melody?
c. Which of these two words does not apply to the next phrase (bars 5–6)?
d. What other word might now be used to describe bars 5–6?
e. How does the final phrase (bars 7–8) differ from the rest of the melody?
f. Does the final phrase share a characteristic with bars 1–4 or bars 5–6?
g. What type of ornament occurs twice during the course of the melody?

◀)) 6 EXERCISE 6

Listen to the melody being played in Track 6. Then answer the following questions:

a. Is the melody in a major or minor key?
b. Which word best describes the contour of the first half of the melody?
c. What direction does the melody move in during the first six bars?
d. How does the contour change at bar 7?
e. What ornament decorates the melody near to the end?
f. What is the interval between the final two notes?

◀)) 7 EXERCISE 7

Listen to the melody being played in Track 7. Then answer the following questions:

a. How many phrases make up this melody?
b. What is the relationship of the second phrase to the first phrase?
c. What is the relationship of the second half of the melody to the first half?
d. What kind of scale has been used to compose this melody?

🔊 8 EXERCISE 8

Listen to the melody being played in Track 8. Then answer the following questions:

a. What elements give the melody and rhythm a strong jazz character in the opening four bars?

b. What device is used in the melody in bar 4?

c. How does the melodic contour differ in the central phrase from what is heard previously? Give three differences.

d. What special playing technique is used for the final note of the melody?

MELODIC DICTATION PRACTICE

One of the questions in Section A is likely to require you to fill in missing notes in a melodic phrase. It may only be four notes that are needed to fill the gap, but with a mark for each note, this seemingly insignificant question is actually 10% of the Section A marks. It is therefore well worth careful, patient practice.

🔊 9–16 EXERCISE 9

The following melody (page 14) is missing its notes for bar 3. There are eight different versions of the bar, which you can hear in Tracks 9–16. In each case there are four notes in the empty bar; the rhythm is always two quavers plus two crotchets.

Listen to each version **three** times and fill in the missing notes.

NOTE

There are three factors to consider:

■ The link from the last note of bar 2 to the first missing note – is it the same, lower or higher in pitch?

■ The shape of the melodic contour in bar 3 – rising or falling, conjunct or disjunct?

■ The link from the last note you write in bar 3 to the written note in bar 4 – the same, lower or higher in pitch?

You may like to consider one factor on each hearing.

This skill offers a great opportunity for teamwork revision: write your own four-bar phrase (keep it simple!) with different versions of the third bar and then challenge a fellow student to work out the various contours you play to him or her.

Then get ready to deal with the return favour!

HARMONY

We now move on to consider aspects of harmony that you may be required to spot aurally in Section A. Often harmony requires, quite literally, a deeper level of listening. Whereas the rhythm and melody are frequently heard on the surface – the top strand of the texture – harmony is usually governed by the bass line and formed by the notes in the middle of the texture. However, it is this very depth to which harmony reaches that often makes it one of the most profound and expressive elements in music. Training the ear to hear harmony is therefore a way to appreciate music more richly.

The next set of exercises are designed to help you recognise the following harmonic features:

consonant, dissonant, major, minor, modal, passing note, auxiliary note, appoggiatura, suspension, pedal note, cadences, tierce de Picardie, modulation, harmonic rhythm.

🔊17 EXERCISE 10

Listen to the music in Track 17. Then answer the following questions:

a. What word best describes the tonality of the music?
b. What type of note decorates the third chord of the piece?
c. What kind of cadence occurs halfway through at the end of the first phrase?
d. What kind of note decorates the first chord of the second phrase?
e. What kind of cadence ends the piece? Identify the final three chords.
f. Does the music end in the same key as it started in?

🔊18 EXERCISE 11

Listen to the music in Track 18. Then answer the following questions:

a. What word best describes the tonality of this music?
b. What harmonic device is heard at the start?
c. A similar device occurs at the start of the second phrase. How is it different this time?
d. Does the music end in the same key as it started in?
e. What cadence occurs at the end of the piece?
f. What device is used in the final chord?

🔊19 EXERCISE 12

Listen to the music in Track 19. Then answer the following questions:

a. What word best describes the first chord you hear? (The second chord, two bars later, is the same chord but an octave lower.)
b. What harmonic pattern underpins the main melody that comes after the four-bar introduction?
c. What kind of cadence finishes the main section (i.e. just before the silent pause)?
d. The music begins in C major. In which key does it finish?
e. What kind of cadence comes at the very end?

🔊20 EXERCISE 13

Listen to the music in Track 20. Then answer the following questions:

a. What word best describes the tonality of this music?
b. How does the note in the melody decorate the first chord? (The third, fifth and seventh chords are all decorated in a similar way.)
c. What is significant about how the harmony changes in the third phrase?
d. How is the final chord decorated?

TEXTURE

Many people find the vocabulary for texture challenging to use, but the differences in texture that exist in music are usually fairly clear to hear. The following exercise should help you to identify textures that are:

> *homophonic, contrapuntal, melody with accompaniment, antiphonal, fugal and canonic.*

The exercises also incorporate other issues already met in this chapter.

🔊21 EXERCISE 14

Listen to the music in Track 21. Then answer the following questions:

a. What is the best description of the texture of this piece?
b. What change occurs in the texture for the second phrase?
c. What is the interval between the first two notes of the melody? Phrases 2 and 3 both begin with the same interval.
d. What ornament occurs during the melody in the second phrase?
e. What type of cadence comes at the end of the third phrase (which is the penultimate phrase)?
f. What type of cadence finishes the piece?

🔊22 EXERCISE 15

Listen to the music in Track 22. Then answer the following questions:

a. What is the best description of the texture of this piece?
b. What word best describes the tonality of the piece?
c. What is significant about the texture halfway through the piece, when the dynamic changes to *f*?
d. What type of cadence finishes the piece?
e. What type of ornament is used in the melody during the final cadence?
f. What type of ornament is used on the final note of the piece (in the bass)?

🔊23 EXERCISE 16

Listen to the music in Track 23. Then answer the following questions:

a. What is the best description of the texture of this piece?
b. What word best describes the tonality of the piece?
c. The music begins in F major; in which key does it finish?
d. What is the metre (time signature) of the music?
e. What rhythmic device is used at the end?
f. What type of cadence finishes the piece?

◀))24 EXERCISE 17

Listen to the music in Track 24. Then answer the following questions:

a. What is the best description of the texture of this piece?
b. What is the metre of the music?
c. What rhythmic device is used after the first phrase?
d. What melodic and harmonic device is used in the second half?
e. The music starts in A♭ major; in which key does it finish?
f. What device is used in the final chord?

◀))25 EXERCISE 18

Listen to the music in Track 25. Then answer the following questions:

a. What is the best description of the texture of this piece?
b. How many times during the course of the piece do you hear the opening melodic idea played?
c. What is significant about the way this melodic idea is played on its last appearance (in the bass just before the end)?
d. What is the tonality of the piece?
e. What type of cadence finishes the piece?
f. What device decorates the final chord?

◀))26 EXERCISE 19

Listen to the music in Track 26. Then answer the following questions:

a. Which **two** words describe the texture of this piece?
b. What harmonic progression underpins the passage of longer legato phrases in the middle of the piece?
c. When the opening theme returns near the end, how is it different from before?

INSTRUMENTATION AND TIMBRE

It is very likely that some of the Section A marks will be for identifying some aspects of instrumentation in the excerpts you hear. Often this involves orchestral music.

If you have played for years in an orchestra, this should be very straightforward. If not, the only way to be sure of securing these marks is to have enough experience of orchestral music. It cannot be done through reading a book or making copious revision notes.

So try to attend some orchestral concerts. Exam preparation never gets more enjoyable than this! It need not be expensive. A number of top-class performance venues often sell standby tickets to students for as little as £5.

If you live too far from a concert hall for this to be a possibility, and you need to improve your recognition of instrumental timbres from home, then no one can help you better than

Benjamin Britten and his *Variations and Fugue on a Theme of Purcell*, better known as *The Young Person's Guide to the Orchestra*. You can find it in Rhinegold Education's YouTube playlist for this book in two parts:

Part 1 at:

Part 2 at:

Here, you can link the sounds with the instruments you see on screen. Then concentrate on just listening and make sure you know which instrument is which.

NOTE

Britten starts with the full orchestral sound and then skilfully deconstructs it into instrumental families (strings, woodwinds, brass, percussion). Next he goes through each family a second time, introducing each member with its own variation. Finally he puts the orchestra back together, instrument by instrument, in a dazzling fugue – starting with the piccolo.

When listening to the work, don't just concentrate on the leading instrument(s) for each variation: listen to the accompaniment too and work out what is being used to support each star turn. Britten's orchestration is highly skilled in this way too.

 EXERCISE 20

This exercise is a test of your ability to identify woodwind and brass instruments in an orchestral piece.

First, listen to the recording of the third movement (Adagio) of Rachmaninov's second symphony conducted by Vladimir Ashkenazy. This is available on YouTube (audio only).

Listen to the first two-and-a-half minutes: there is a very beautiful and long clarinet solo, and – at the start – this arched figure is heard in the violins:

You may wish to take the time to listen to the whole movement (the climax midway is well worth it), but this exercise now moves to the recapitulation much later in the movement.

For this access the fourth clip in the YouTube playlist and the passage starting at 1:13.

Here the long melody that was played before by the solo clarinet is now played by the first violins, and around it the original violin figure is played 11 times before the long theme is completed at 3:16. Listen carefully, and note down which instrument plays the arched figure each of the 11 times it appears.

In actual fact the arch motif occurs throughout much of the movement, and there are plenty of other appearances of it elsewhere for you to spot the instrument (including some not covered in the above exercise), so you can enjoy the whole movement!

Instrumentation and timbre is a vast topic, and a book of this scope can only give you a few pointers: it is up to you to gain the real-life experience of how each instrument sounds to you. It is not unlike learning the names we give to colours: quite how would you teach someone the difference between red and orange, blue and purple, without actually showing them the colours? So you need to listen (not just hear) as much instrumental music as possible.

In particular, listen for:

- Orchestras: the different instruments and playing techniques ranging from mutes (strings and brass) to flutter-tonguing (woodwinds) and pizzicato and col legno (strings).
- Jazz ensembles: the various different kinds of saxophones, bass instruments, drumkit sounds and specialist trumpet and trombone mutes.
- Pop music: different guitar effects and the sounds generated and edited electronically.
- Singers: different voice types from coloratura soprano to contralto and countertenor to bass, and specialist singing techniques such as scat singing.

Revising this section should be pure fun!

Specimen questions

There are usually two types of question in Section A.

- Questions 1–3 are similar: essentially purely aural, short-answer questions. One of the questions will probably include notation for part of the melody with some notes missing that you have to fill in (as on page 14). It is possible that one of the questions might involve two different pieces of music being played to you.
- Question 4 is usually different. You will still hear the music played, but there will also be a score of the music, which in the past has been an orchestral piece. This allows the examiners to ask more location-specific questions and will test your skills for score-reading, including handling transposing instruments.

The answers and comments to the specimen questions can be found on pages 80–83.

FOUR 'AURAL ONLY' QUESTIONS

Suggested recordings from YouTube are provided in Rhinegold Education's YouTube playlist, as well as advice on locating the correct passage from other sources. You should play the excerpts the number of times stated in the questions, with a gap of 20 seconds between each playing.

QUESTION 1

You will hear an excerpt from Mozart's *Kegelstatt Trio* K. 498. The music will be played four times with pauses between each playing.

> **NOTE**
>
> Recommended recording:
>
>
>
> Stop at 1:46.
>
> If you are listening to a recording from a different source, it is the first movement (Trio) up to bar 35.

a. Which string instrument plays with the piano at the start? *(1 mark)*
b. Which ornament features as part of the main motif that is heard many times: acciaccatura, mordent, trill or turn? *(1 mark)*
c. Which wind instrument enters in bar 9? *(1 mark)*
d. What kind of scale does this instrument play at the end of its first phrase? *(2 marks)*
e. What is the tonality of this music? *(1 mark)*
f. A second theme is introduced by the wind instrument after two slow piano chords. What key is this theme played in: dominant, relative major, relative minor or subdominant? *(1 mark)*
g. What is the best description of the texture of this new section: canonic, contrapuntal, homophonic, or melody with accompaniment? *(1 mark)*
h. What cadence is heard at the end of the excerpt? *(1 mark)*
i. Give a suitable time signature for the piece. *(1 mark)*

Total: 10 marks

QUESTION 2

You will hear an excerpt from Malcolm Arnold's *English Dances* Set 2, No. 3, 'Grazioso'. The music will be played four times with pauses between each playing.

> **NOTE**
>
> Recommended recording:
>
>
>
> Start at 4:34; stop at 5:56.
>
> If you are listening to a recording from a different source, start at the beginning of the third dance and stop at the end of the third time through the melody, as the trumpets enter.

a. The music is built over a repeating pattern of two chords. Which percussion instrument is involved with the chords? *(1 mark)*

b. What is the interval between the bass notes of the chords: 3rd, 4th, 5th or 6th? *(1 mark)*

c. Complete the empty bar in the oboe melody by filling in the four missing quavers. *(4 marks)*

d. Which instruments play the melody after the oboe? *(2 marks)*

e. The strings then take over the melody. How is the texture different at this point? *(1 mark)*

f. What is the tonality of the music? *(1 mark)*

Total: 10 marks

QUESTION 3

You will hear an excerpt from a sonata by César Franck. The music will be played four times with pauses between each playing.

> **NOTE**
>
> Recommended recording (with Jascha Heifitz and Arthur Rubinstein):
>
>
>
> Stop at 0:55.
>
> If you are listening to a recording from a different source, it is the opening of the fourth movement of the sonata (Allegretto ben moderato) up to bar 37.

a. What is the solo instrument that the piano is accompanying? *(1 mark)*

b. How is the instrument being played: arco, col legno, pizzicato or sul ponticello? *(1 mark)*

c. Complete the first phrase of the melody below by filling in the missing notes. *(4 marks)*

d. Which **one** of the following best describes the melody at the start: chromatic, diatonic, pentatonic or whole tone? *(1 mark)*

e. What is the texture of the music: canonic, fugal, heterophonic, or melody with accompaniment? *(1 mark)*

f. What cadence is heard at the end of the excerpt? *(1 mark)*

g. Which **one** of the following statements is true? *(1 mark)*
- The music remains in the same key throughout
- The music ends in the dominant key
- The music ends in the same key as it began
- The music ends in the relative minor.

Total: 10 marks

QUESTION 4

You will hear an excerpt from Tchaikovsky's Symphony No. 4. The music will be played four times with pauses between each playing.

NOTE
Recommended recording: Stop at 1:35. If you are listening to a recording from a different source, it is the second movement up to bar 41 (just before figure A).

a. Which instrument plays the melody at the start? *(1 mark)*
b. What term best describes the playing technique heard in the strings? *(1 mark)*
c. What is the tonality of the music? *(1 mark)*
d. The main melody is repeated by part of the string section. Which instruments play it: violins, violas, cellos or double basses? *(1 mark)*
e. At this point there is a countermelody on two clarinets. Which description best fits their phrase? *(1 mark)*
- A rising arpeggio in unison
- A rising arpeggio in octaves
- A rising scale in unison
- A rising scale in octaves.
f. The countermelody then passes to another woodwind instrument. Which instrument? *(1 mark)*
g. Which **three** of the following can be heard in the excerpt? *(3 marks)*
- Circle of 5ths harmony
- Hemiola
- Imperfect cadence
- Ostinato
- Plagal cadence
- Sequence
- Tierce de Picardie.

h. Give a suitable time signature. *(1 mark)*

Total: 10 marks

TWO 'WITH SCORE' QUESTIONS

Scores for these questions are provided on the book companion website at www.rhinegoldeducation.co.uk: see log in details on page 4.

QUESTION 5

You will hear an excerpt from the third movement of Haydn's Symphony No. 89. The music will be played twice with a pause between the playings.

NOTE

Recommended recording:

Stop at 1:31.

If you are listening to a recording from a different source, it is the Menuet section of the third movement, stopping where the Trio starts.

a. Complete this sentence to describe the texture in the opening four-bar phrase: "There is a _ _ _ _ _-part texture doubled at _ _ _ _ _ _ different octaves. *(2 marks)*

b. What compositional technique does Haydn use in bars 4^3 to 6^2? *(1 mark)*

c. In what key does the music cadence at bar 12? *(1 mark)*

d. What harmonic device is used in bars 8–12? *(1 mark)*

e. Which instruments continue this device in bars 13–16? *(2 marks)*

f. At what interval apart are the violas and cellos between bars 28^3 and 31^1: 2nd, 3rd, 5th or 6th? *(1 mark)*

g. Give a bar and beat number where the first horn sounds higher than the first oboe for the duration of the entire beat. *(1 mark)*

h. In what form is this excerpt: binary, rondo, sonata or ternary? *(1 mark)*

Total: 10 marks

QUESTION 6

You will hear an excerpt from the first movement of Reicha's Wind Quintet in C major Op. 91 No. 1. The music will be played three times with a pause between the playings.

> **NOTE**
>
> Recommended recording:
>
>
>
> Stop at 1:26.
>
> If you are listening to a recording from a different source, it is the start of the Quintet, stopping on the downbeat of bar 39.

a. What ornament does the oboe play in bars 4 and 6? *(1 mark)*
b. Describe fully the chord marked **X** in bar 8. *(2 marks)*
c. Describe fully the chord marked **Y** in bar 8. *(2 marks)*
d. What key does the music change to for the Andante section? *(1 mark)*
e. What harmonic progression occurs in bars 18–21? *(1 mark)*
f. What ornament does the flute play in bar 25? *(1 mark)*
g. What interval apart are the flute and clarinet in bars 34–35? *(1 mark)*
h. Identify a bar in which the horn sounds lower than the bassoon. *(1 mark)*

Total: 10 marks

Unit 1 – Section B: Historical Study – Area of Study 1 (set work)

This section of the exam is based on your study of the set work: Haydn's Symphony No. 104, movements 1 and 3. It tests your analytical understanding of the music and your ability to write well about the piece. You will need to choose examples from the music to suit a given question, and describe the construction and effect of the music with confidence, using technical vocabulary.

The material here is designed to help you prepare for this section of the exam, and comes in two halves:

■ Firstly, there is advice on structuring your revision notes. This provides you with ready examples for some passages of the symphony, and then encourages you to produce similar material for the rest of the two movements set by AQA.

■ Secondly, we look at AQA's mark scheme and some example essay questions and answers, in order to gain an examiner's insight into what makes for a good essay for this exam.

NOTE

Completing your own revision notes will in itself be an excellent way of revising, especially if you follow the examples given below.

Making revision notes

THE AIM

For your set-work study, you will have analysed the first and third movements from Haydn's 104th symphony (the 'London Symphony').

In the exam there will be two essay questions from which you choose **one** to answer. These questions are numbered 5 and 6 on the exam paper. You will have about 35 minutes to write your essay, which will then be marked out of 20.

It is likely that question 5 will be based on the first movement of the symphony, while question 6 will ask something about the third movement. However, make sure you read the questions carefully: it is possible that a question could refer to both movements.

Commonly, there are two types of question:

1. Write in detail about one passage of music with reference to all elements of music. For example: '*Write an informative account of the introduction in the first movement of this symphony. You should refer to structure, melody, texture, instrumentation, rhythm, harmony and tonality.*'

2. Write about an entire movement with reference to just one (or maybe two) elements of music. For example: '*Describe the ways in which Haydn makes use of rhythm in the third movement of this symphony.*'

In either style of question it is easy to be drawn off course. In the first you can find yourself writing about music from elsewhere in the movement; in the second it is easy to spend time writing about elements other than the one set by the question. 35 minutes is not long for writing an answer to either question, and you cannot afford to spend 5 minutes writing a very interesting paragraph about something that lies outside the scope of the question. You will not get any marks for such a paragraph.

In order to practise writing essays of the kind you will need to write in the exam room, it is recommended that you organise your revision notes according to the following tables. In these tables, the boxes with ticks are those for which example revision notes can be found below. As you compile your own notes for the other boxes you can tick them off; this way you can see at a glance how much there is still left to do.

FIRST MOVEMENT

	Introduction	Exposition	Development	Recapitulation/coda
Structure	✓			
Melody	✓			
Rhythm	✓			
Harmony	✓	✓	✓	✓
Texture	✓			
Instrumentation	✓			

THIRD MOVEMENT

	Minuet section A	Minuet section B	Trio section A	Trio section B
Structure				✓
Melody				✓
Rhythm	✓	✓	✓	✓
Harmony				✓
Texture				✓
Instrumentation				✓

To revise with maximum thoroughness, you should aim to have a separate page of revision notes for each box in the grid. At the top left corner of the page put the section of the movement:

FIRST MOVEMENT: EXPOSITION

and at the top right corner of the page put the element:

INSTRUMENTATION

Then, if you are writing an essay on the exposition in the first movement, you can use all of the pages labelled 'First movement: exposition' to write the essay, and *limit yourself to the facts you have on those pages*. Similarly, if you are writing about instrumentation in the second movement, use the relevant revision notes as your guide to what to write.

There will not necessarily be an equal amount to say for the topic represented by each box. Make sure that you only include in your revision notes:

■ Relevant points
■ Good-quality points
■ Points that you fully understand.

This also means that you can revise methodically, concentrating one session on 'Texture' and the next on 'Second movement: exposition' for instance. This way, your revision will look at each page of score from different angles and be all the more thorough for it.

NOTE

As a refinement to this system, you may wish to use different colour paper for the two movements. A third colour could be used for your Section C notes.

Not every page of revision notes will have an equal amount of information: there may be more to say about the exposition than the coda, or about the melody than the texture in some sections of the work. Set out the information spaciously, so it is easy to remember each point at a glance. Make sure important points are linked to specific examples in the score with bar-number references.

FIRST MOVEMENT: INTRODUCTION – STRUCTURE

Overview

Haydn's London Symphony will be full of charm, elegance and sparkle; however, he uses the introduction to create an arresting and serious start that also has a sense of mystery. This is achieved by beginning in D minor rather than D major and by starting with an Adagio tempo marking.

The 16 bars that make up the introduction alternate between a simple fanfare idea played loudly, and a less confident, quiet idea.

Fanfare idea

The fanfare idea appears three times:

- Bars 1–2 in D minor
- Bars 7–8 in F (the relative major)
- Bars 14–15 back in D minor.

The arresting, fanfare quality is due to the:

- Full orchestra playing in octaves
- Use of a double dotted rhythm on repeated notes
- Leap of a 5th from tonic to dominant
- Timpani rolls.

Further details to note include:

- Bar 2 answers bar 1 by falling from the tonic to dominant instead of rising.
- At bars 7–8 the brass and timpani are silent (as they cannot play the notes F and C), which helps to make D more important than F as the tonic for the piece.
- At bars 14–15 the second bar now falls to the subdominant. Haydn highlights the change by reducing the dynamic to *pp* and introducing the Neapolitan chord at bar 8^4.

Secondary idea

The music between appearances of the fanfare figure is mysterious in quality due to the:

- Quiet dynamic and reduced scoring
- Confirmation of the minor tonality after the ambiguous open 5th of bars 1–2
- Double dotted pattern now moving by step rather than leaping upwards
- Frequent use of first-inversion chords
- Use of chromatic colour.

FIRST MOVEMENT: INTRODUCTION – MELODY

The melodies of the introduction are motivic in nature and contrast between:

1. The fanfare idea which:
   - Rises by an assertive leap of a 5th
   - That is answered by a falling 4th, which complements the opening leap while maintaining the tonic-to-dominant identity.
2. The secondary idea which:
   - Falls by step (often a semitone)
   - Uses a nervous staccato reiteration of the final note in the bar.

There is also a chromatic countermelody in the first violins at bar 12.

FIRST MOVEMENT: INTRODUCTION – RHYTHM

The introduction adopts a slow tempo (Adagio) and a sense of formality from the $\frac{4}{4}$ metre.

The most distinctive rhythmic feature is the double dotted pattern in the fanfare idea.

This is echoed in the quieter passages. Here some of the instruments enter after a quaver rest (e.g. first violin bar 3), creating a sense of unease as a result of the displacement.

FIRST MOVEMENT: INTRODUCTION – HARMONY

Bars 1–2

The fanfare idea is heard in octaves (without harmony) but strongly gives a tonic-dominant context. The lack of a third keeps open the option to be in either D major or D minor.

Bars 3–6

The arrival of an F in the bass clarifies the key as D minor.

It is also significant that the harmony here uses inversions of the tonic and dominant chords, whereas the octaves of bars 1–2 present the roots (only) of tonic and dominant. These inversions are less stable and, coupled with the minor tonality, give the music its sense of mystery.

Note how the third bar of this progression promises to be the same as the previous two, but small changes in the harmony (C natural instead of C♯ in the violin; B♭ rather than A in the viola and bassoon) moves the music away from D minor to its relative major of F major:

Bars 7–8

The fanfare idea returns but moved up a 3rd to suggest F major, the relative major.

Bars 9–13

This passage inhabits the same musical world as bars 3–6, although it is a bit quieter. However, the mood of suspense is heightened. Haydn achieves this by:

- An increased use of chromaticism that gives some sense of tonal uncertainty
- A rising sequence in bars 9–11
- The melodic motif occurring more frequently from bar 11.

Bar 13 brings the music back to the home key of D minor, which is reached with a Ic–V⁷–I perfect cadence on to the downbeat of bar 14.

Bars 14–16

The fanfare idea returns in D minor, but with a twist in bar 15. Here Haydn uses the Neapolitan chord (the chord on the flattened second, i.e. E♭).

By ending with an imperfect cadence (on chord V⁷), Haydn can immediately start the Allegro in D major (since A⁷ is the dominant 7th of both D minor and D major).

FIRST MOVEMENT: INTRODUCTION – TEXTURE

The fanfare idea is always presented in an octave texture.

The secondary idea has a homophonic texture, with an element of dialogue between the second violins in the first half of the bar and the first violins in the second half of the bar.

At bar 12 the main melody passes into the bass line (played by the cellos), with a countermelody in the violins.

FIRST MOVEMENT: INTRODUCTION – INSTRUMENTATION

Fanfare idea

The fanfare idea is heard as an orchestral tutti in bars 1–2.

At bars 7–8 the brass and timpani do not play due to the limitations they would have faced in the Classical period (brass had no valves; timpani could only play one note each).

At bars 14–15 the strings alone play the second bar, to aid the *pp* effect.

Secondary material

Bars 3–6 are mainly played by strings, with bassoon doubling the violas for a little extra colour and sonority.

At bars 9–13 the scoring is initially the same, until the introduction of the flute in bar 12 provides some additional warmth.

The solo oboe line at bar 16 creates a plaintive effect.

FIRST MOVEMENT: EXPOSITION – HARMONY

First subject (bars 17–50)

The harmony here is purely diatonic.

In true Classical fashion, the first eight-bar phrase ends with an imperfect cadence and the second with a perfect cadence.

The descending bass line in bars 20–23 lends the music elegance, and the second violins here have a series of 7-6 suspensions.

The second phrase complements the first one by including a rising bass line.

The tutti from bar 32 alternates chords I and IVc to maintain a tonic pedal note.

There is greater sophistication in the harmony from bar 40, with a change in the harmonic rhythm (two bars per chord) and chromatic lower auxiliaries in both the melody and bass line, decorating chords VI and IV.

Transition (bars 50–64)

Further chromatic colour here allows Haydn to modulate with some subtlety towards the dominant key of A, ending on the chord of E major: the new dominant.

Second subject (bars 65–99)

The reworking of the first subject at this point (creating a monothematic movement) involves further chromaticism from bar 73, which gives the music some contrast at this point.

As the second subject becomes tutti at bar 86, Haydn returns to a I–IVc–I pattern.

Five bars of a dominant pedal (from bar 92) preface the main cadence at the end of the second subject.

Closing theme (bars 99–123)

This passage begins with a tonic pedal in the horns.

The tutti at bar 112 is again built on a I–IVc–I progression.

The exposition ends with a flourish over a tonic pedal (bars 120–123).

FIRST MOVEMENT: DEVELOPMENT – HARMONY

Bars 124–145

The development immediately moves to the relative minor (B minor) via an F♯⁷ chord in bar 124.

The music then soon moves to E minor at bar 127.

From bar 141, with the B♮s changing to B♯s as part of a G♯⁷ chord, the music moves towards C♯ minor.

Bars 145–155

This passage begins in C♯ minor and then travels round the circle of 5ths in a descending sequence:

| in C♯ minor | in G♯ minor | in F♯ minor | in E major |

Bars 155–179

After passing through various minor keys in the previous section, Haydn marks the arrival on to E major at bar 155 with an f tutti section. However, after two bars of E major, the G♯s are swapped for G♮s as he heads back into E minor at bar 157 for an extended passage in this key.

Bars 170–171 use a first-inversion E minor chord (which was the tonality of the preceding passage). Then in bars 172–173, Haydn swaps the E♮ for an E♯, which produces the interval of an augmented 6th above the G in the bass. This augmented 6th chord has a strong need to resolve, with the G descending and the E♯ ascending, both by a semitone on to F♯:

E minor 1st inversion ⟶ Augmented 6th chord ⟶ F♯ major

This progression moves the music away from E minor. The impetus of the resolution on to F♯ makes this sound like a new dominant, which is underlined by five bars of F♯ as a pedal note. On the downbeat of bar 179, this delivers the music into the key of B minor.

Bars 179–192

From B minor (the relative minor of the home key), the music reaches a dominant pedal (A) in bar 185, to herald the return to D major and the recapitulation.

FIRST MOVEMENT: RECAPITULATION – HARMONY

First subject (bars 193–243)

The music here is similar to the exposition and shares the following elements:

- A diatonic presentation of the main theme
- Use of I–IVc–I patterns in the tutti section from bar 208
- A slower harmonic rhythm and chromatic decoration of chords VI and IV from bar 216.

From bar 220 there is a new passage to ensure that the music does not modulate again towards the dominant (as it did in the exposition). The harmony here is based on the circle of 5ths:

Second subject (bars 244–266)

The imitative entries of the head motif (the opening four notes of the first subject) are based on tonic harmony, before some chromatic inflections are heard as part of a short circle of 5ths passage in bars 253–256.

The tutti at bar 257 again uses chords VI and IV, but with a faster (two chords per bar) harmonic rhythm.

Closing theme (bars 266–277)

This is essentially the same as the music of the exposition, now transposed into D major.

Coda (bar 277–294)

A totally diatonic passage of music, but with some agile changes of harmonic rhythm.

THIRD MOVEMENT: MINUET SECTION A – RHYTHM

The music has many of the hallmarks of the minuet style:

- An Allegro tempo
- A $\frac{3}{4}$ time signature
- An anacrusis to start.

Haydn brings extra rhythmic character to the music with the staccato crotchets on beats 1 and 2 of the bar, and the *sf* markings on beat 3.

Cadences are stylised; the whole orchestra plays a dotted minim in the penultimate bar of each eight-bar phrase, and many of the parts have a trill at this point.

THIRD MOVEMENT: MINUET SECTION B – RHYTHM

As a complementary second half to the minuet, it is not surprising that the rhythmic character of section B is consistent with section A. Additional features include:

- The sense of hemiola in the bass line during bars 21–24
- A melody in flowing quavers in bars 23–25
- Two bars of trill (rather than the one bar in Section A) at bars 47–48.

THIRD MOVEMENT: TRIO SECTION A – RHYTHM

The metre and tempo remain the same as for the minuet.

Contrast with the minuet is immediately created by the first downbeat being a minim rather than repeated staccato crotchets.

The main melodic idea is then a long line of flowing quavers (which was foreshadowed in section B of the minuet at bar 23). Simple rhythmic patterns are given to the pizzicato chords underneath to maintain the sense of the triple-time dance.

THIRD MOVEMENT: TRIO SECTION B – STRUCTURE

Bars 65–78

There is some sense of development here, as Haydn explores various combinations of the rising 3rd and flowing quavers that began the trio, while passing through various keys (C minor, G minor, F major).

Bars 79–83

The return to B♭ major and the trio's opening phrase creates a rounded binary structure for the trio.

Bars 84–87

A descending line in the flute twists the music towards the subdominant – thus avoiding the original modulation towards the dominant (which is only needed in the first half of a binary form).

Bars 88–94

After a general pause, a final graceful phrase concludes the main trio section.

Bars 95–104

Haydn provides an additional phrase to ease the return from B♭ major back to D major for the da capo of the minuet.

THIRD MOVEMENT: TRIO SECTION B – MELODY

The melodic material here is based on:

- The rising 3rd figure
- Running legato quaver lines
- The falling chromatic line in the flute at bar 84.

THIRD MOVEMENT: TRIO SECTION B – RHYTHM

Rhythmically, this section continues with elements already met in the movement:

- Use of an anacrusis beat
- Crotchet-minim patterns
- Long lines of quavers.

In the additional phrase from bar 95, Haydn prepares for the return of the minuet by:

- Avoiding the quavers
- Using repeating crotchets in the bass line (played by violas).

THIRD MOVEMENT: TRIO SECTION B – HARMONY

Bars 65–78

Having cadenced in F major at the end of section A, Haydn immediately heads in a different direction, reintroducing E♭s and swapping the A♮s for A♭s.

This takes the music towards C minor at bar 67, and then F♯s are introduced to suggest G minor. However, at bar 72 B♮s and A♭s take us back towards C minor.

The lack of a strong tonal anchor makes it easy for Haydn to then treat C minor as the supertonic, as he heads back to the trio's tonic of B♭ major at bar 79.

This passage has some expressive harmony, with the downbeats of bars 66 and 73 both using dominant minor 9th chords (G in the bass, A♭ in the melody).

Bars 79–87

The return of the trio's opening phrase uses the I–V^{7}c–V^7–I progression that was so common in the Classical era.

The falling chromatic line in the flute at bars 84–86 turns the tonic harmony into a secondary dominant 7th chord – V^7 of IV – and the harmony then moves on to chord IV, to leave a sense of necessary resolution hanging in the air at the general pause.

Bars 88–94

The final phrase is essentially IIb–V–I, but this is decorated with rising chromatic inflections first in the viola and then in the cello, which echo the previous falling chromatic line in the flute. The perfect cadence is also elaborated with a Ic–V progression in bar 93.

Bars 95–104

Chromatic lines continue in this additional phrase. These enable Haydn to turn the chord of B♭ major into an augmented 6th chord (B♭ in the bass, G♯ in the first violins) at bar 99. This then demands resolution on to A major, which sets up the return to D major and the da capo of the minuet.

THIRD MOVEMENT: TRIO SECTION B – TEXTURE

Bars 65–78

The quavers that formed the upper melodic line to the texture in section A now move to the bass line in a two-part contrapuntal texture.

At bars 72–74, a G pedal note (V in C minor) provides a third part to the texture, before the quavers return to the melodic line in bar 75.

Bars 79–94

The return of the trio opening has the same melody-and-accompaniment texture as before.

After the general pause, the rising-3rd shape returns in an octave texture for two bars.

Bars 95–104

This is a homophonic passage built over two pedal notes:

- Bars 95–99: a tonic pedal in B♭ major.
- Bars 100–104: a dominant pedal in D major.

THIRD MOVEMENT: TRIO SECTION B – INSTRUMENTATION

There is a constantly changing blend of strings and woodwinds here:

- The first-violin quavers are initially doubled an octave below by the bassoon and then in unison by the oboe.
- The quavers then appear in 6ths on second violins and violas.
- The crotchet-minim melody is initially played by solo flute (at bar 66), and then taken by first violins and bassoon in octaves.

The return of the trio opening is, as before, accompanied by pizzicato lower strings, but here the bassoons gently reinforce the chords.

The additional phrase linking back to the minuet is *p* but has a richness with all lines played by strings and winds.

Throughout the brass and timpani are silent, waiting to play again with the return to D major in the minuet da capo.

Writing essays

ACCESSING THE MARKS

Your essays will be assessed for the following qualities:

- Knowledge and understanding of the music
- Relevance to the question set
- Points supported by references to the score
- Specialist vocabulary
- Awareness of context
- Writing style.

Bearing these factors in mind, you can see that you want to avoid the following pitfalls:

- Factual inaccuracies and inaccurate analytical comments
- Writing about aspects of the piece that are not relevant to the question
- Making general points that are not backed up by specific references to the score
- Avoiding appropriate technical terms, or using technical vocabulary in incorrect ways
- Writing with poor spelling, grammar and structure in your essay.

Writing good essays requires practice. In particular:

- The more you have studied the piece, the more your analytical understanding will be accurate and comprehensive.
- The more angles you have considered each movement from, the quicker you will locate the specific examples that will support the points you make.
- The more you use specialist vocabulary in conversation, reading about the music, making notes and writing about the piece, the more comfortable and convincing you will be in using technical terms.
- The more practice essays you write, the better your writing style will be and the more confident you will be, helping you to keep to time in the exam.

Therefore, make sure you factor into your revision schedule times when you will practise writing essays.

NOTE

Past papers and mark schemes for Unit 1 are available to download from the AQA website. These can be very useful for exam practice, and will help to give you a better idea of what the examiners are looking for in your answers.

Read the following essay as though you were an examiner. Consider the various factors listed above. Can you see any shortcomings? What mark out of 20 would you award this candidate?

You may like to fill in the table on the next page as you assess this answer.

Write an informative account of the introduction in the first movement of this symphony. You should refer to structure, melody, texture, instrumentation, rhythm, harmony and tonality.

Haydn was born in Austria in 1732. He spent most of his career working for a Prince at Esterhazy, but wrote his final symphony for the London concert scene in 1795 when Salomon invited the great composer to visit Britain. The symphony is written for a large Classical orchestra with a full range of wind instruments as well as trumpets and timpani.

Haydn starts the symphony with a slow introduction, something he had done in many of his previous 103 symphonies. The symphony begins with the full orchestra playing **ff** for two bars, including some exciting drum rolls on the timpani. All instruments are playing the same tune in different octaves. This tune has a strong dotted rhythm pattern. This makes a stirring start to the piece and makes a very grand effect.

The following four bars by contrast are **p** and mysterious. A solo bassoon is supported by the lower strings and the first violins answer in the second half of each bar. This section ends with a perfect cadence in bar 6, which is followed by a repeat of the opening two bars, returning to **ff**, but now at a different pitch.

Haydn then returns to the **p** idea from bar 3, only this time lengthens the phrase to five bars with the inclusion of a solo flute. Also, this time the passage begins with a rising sequence as bar 5 is repeated up a tone in the next bar in order to add interest.

There is one more appearance of the opening **ff** idea at bar 14, only this time there is a surprise as the second bar is suddenly **pp** and played by the strings only. The introduction ends with a Ic to V⁷ cadence. This leaves a sense of suspense which gets resolved when the Allegro starts.

Paragraph	Strengths	Weaknesses
1		
2		
3		
4		
5		

An annotated version of this answer can be found on pages 84–85.

Here is a different answer to the same question. What is your impression of this essay?

Write an informative account of the introduction in the first movement of this symphony. You should refer to structure, melody, texture, instrumentation, rhythm, harmony and tonality.

Writing his final symphony for the London concert platform, Haydn begins with a masterly slow introduction that is both a call to attention and a suspense-building passage. This comes in three subsections. Each of these subsections is announced with a strong, yet simple, melodic idea played forte in an octaves texture by the full orchestra.

At the start, this figure uses the notes D and A – the tonic and dominant notes of the home key (D major). The rising 5th in bar 1 is answered by a falling 4th in bar 2; the slow tempo, loud dynamic and double-dotted rhythm bring a sense of formality to the music. The following four bars are piano and far more discreet, although the double-dotted rhythm is still featured. The harmony confirms the key of D minor, but chords are heard in inversions rather than confident root positions, and all the linear movement is conjunct rather than the bold leaps of bars 1–2. The music is carried by a subtle blend of strings and bassoon (which largely doubles the violas), and gradually modulates towards the relative major.

At bar 7 the opening octaves fanfare returns, but now in F major (and therefore without brass and timpani). The responding phrase is now extended to five bars and is a little more involved in terms of texture and chromaticism, especially from bar 12 where the dotted figure appears in the bass under chromatically shifting harmony that moves the music back to D minor.

Bar 14 is the same as bar 1: the music has returned to D minor. However, the next bar comes as a surprise: the dynamic suddenly drops to *pp* and what was previously a falling 4th (to maintain the tonic to dominant motif) becomes a falling 5th. At bar 15^4 the G is harmonised with an E♭ major chord – the Neapolitan – which creates a rich colour as the music approaches a Ic–V^7 imperfect cadence in bar 16. A plaintive solo oboe emphasises the dominant note, approaching it (in dotted rhythm) from both underneath and above by a semitone.

By breaking off the introduction on an A^7 chord, Haydn sustains a sense of tension through the silence of the general pause. This becomes resolved as the exposition starts in the sunshine of D major and with the free-flowing music of the Allegro.

This answer – only about 20 per cent longer than the first one – is far superior. It shows a comprehensive understanding of the music and confines itself to answering the question. Detailed comments are given with bar (and beat) references, and there is confident use of technical vocabulary. The essay begins with an explanation of the overall structure of the introduction, rather than starting with fine detail. The candidate has shown good awareness of the context, especially in terms of the relationship of the introduction to the whole movement, and there is a mature writing style. The candidate should expect a very high mark.

NOTE

Did you identify the ways in which the answer addresses the elements listed in the question?

- Structure
- Melody
- Texture
- Instrumentation
- Rhythm
- Harmony
- Tonality.

Try listing the vocabulary used in this sample essay that links with each of these elements.

Here is an answer to a different sort of question that requires you to consider a complete movement, but from one angle.

Describe the ways in which Haydn makes use of rhythm in the third movement of this symphony.

Haydn writes a traditional minuet for the third movement, and indicates that this should be played in a lively manner ('Allegro'). By choosing a time signature of ¾ Haydn ensures that the music will have a dance character. Also the music is in D major and begins forte so there is a confident and positive start. The opening plays the same phrase twice, but Haydn shows that the music should be played *piano* second time.

From bar 17 the tune is in crotchets for some time and then the music runs down the scale in quavers for extra energy. The music here is quite chromatic which gives a sense of being the middle of the minuet. For instance, the B♭s from bar 30 mean the music is in F major here. The music then returns to the opening tune. There is a strange break for two bars towards the end of the minuet.

The trio section continues in the same tempo and time signature. There are far more quavers here to create a greater sense of excitement in the music, but also more dotted minims too, as in the flute part at bar 84. The brass and timpani do not play in the trio because it is in a different key. Haydn provides an additional section at the end of the trio to lead back to the minuet which stands out because it does not have any quavers.

How well do you think this candidate has answered the question? Does it do all the things that the examiners are looking for (as listed on page 38)?

Make a list of all the ways in which you could improve this answer. You should be producing quite a long list, because this is not a very good answer. There is some evidence that the candidate has not been able to hear the sound of the music inside their head when looking at the score and writing their essay. What suggests this?

When you have listed all the improvements you can suggest, look at the annotated version of the essay on pages 85–86. Were there any points you overlooked? Now try to write the essay that the candidate should have written.

FURTHER ESSAY TITLES

Here are some additional essay questions for you to try:

1. Give a detailed analysis of the exposition of the first movement. You should refer to melody, harmony and tonality, texture, and instrumentation.
2. In the first movement, how does Haydn use harmony and tonality to build the development section?
3. Describe the ways in which Haydn explores melody and texture in the development section of the first movement.
4. In the first movement of this symphony, how does the recapitulation differ from the exposition?
5. Write an informative account of the minuet section of the third movement of this symphony. You should refer to structure, melody, texture, instrumentation, rhythm, harmony and tonality.
6. In what ways does the trio section of the third movement provide a contrast to the main minuet section?
7. Describe the ways in which Haydn writes for the horns, trumpets and timpani in both the first and third movements of this symphony.

Unit 1 - Section C: Historical Study - Area of Study 2 (selected topic)

The final section of the Unit 1 exam is based on your selected historical topic. You will have been learning about music from one of the following topics:

- Choral Music in the Baroque Period
- Music Theatre From 1940 to 1980
- British Popular Music From 1960 to the Present Day.

For each of these topics there will be two essay titles on the exam paper, and you only have to answer **one** question from the topic you have been studying.

In part, this is a similar challenge to the one met in Section B: a test of your ability to write well on the music you have been studying, giving good analytical detail and making use of appropriate technical vocabulary, in a way that is clearly relevant to the question you are answering.

There is, however, an extra dimension here. In Section B, where all candidates have been studying the same piece, you are allowed a copy of the score with you in the exam room. In Section C, where there are no set works and so you and your teacher have had the opportunity to select your own choice of music representative of the topic, you are not allowed to take scores into the exam. This means that Section C is also a test of your musical memory. Without the visual aid of a score to turn to, you will need to be able to recall the sound of the music in your inner ear unprompted. It is therefore very important that you factor into your revision timetable plenty of opportunity for listening to the music you have been studying in this area.

Since, across the country, a wide range of music will have been studied for these three topics, it is not possible for a book of this scope to cover every piece that you may have been looking at for your selected topic. You will need to refer to your own notes, and any textbook you have been using through the course, to remind yourself of the important facts and analysis that you have covered.

What you will find in this section is some advice for each topic on how to prepare your revision notes for this section and how to make sure you have covered a wide enough range of music for your chosen topic. There is also some advice on essay writing, and a sample essay for you to assess as though you were an examiner.

The marking of Section C essays is very similar to Section B. Examiners will be looking for the following strengths in your essay:

- Sound knowledge and understanding of the music
- Clear relevance to the question set
- Specific points supported by references to the score
- Correct and confident use of specialist vocabulary
- An awareness of context
- A mature writing style.

If you have been working on music theatre, turn to page 48. If you have chosen British popular music, turn to page 52. The section on Baroque choral music follows on straightaway. Annotated versions of the sample answers to these questions can be found on pages 87–93.

Area of Study 2a: Choral Music in the Baroque Period

ORGANISING YOUR REVISION NOTES

You need to be prepared for questions that can come from three angles:

- Types of movement: choruses, arias, recitatives

  Example: Choose two contrasting arias from the music you have studied, and write informatively about each.

- Different moods of music, as suggested by the lyrics and realised in the music

  *Example: How did Baroque composers convey a mood of majesty in their choral music? Refer to **at least two** different pieces of music in your answer.*

- Different composers

  *Example: Contrast music by **two** different composers of the Baroque period, highlighting aspects of their choral writing.*

In each case the question may steer you to talk about one or two elements of music only, such as melody, harmony and tonality, rhythm, texture, or use of voices.

*Example: Choose **two** contrasting movements by the **same** composer and write about the way harmony and texture are used.*

Bearing all these aspects in mind, it would be a good idea to organise your revision notes for this section in a methodical manner so that you have a systematic approach to learning information about different pieces that might combine to answer one of these questions.

Use a separate piece of paper for each movement you have studied, and organise it in a way that will allow you to separate out all the different elements. For example:

TITLE OF MOVEMENT	
Composer:	
Chorus / Aria / Recitative:	
Mood:	
Structure	
Melody	
Harmony / tonality	
Rhythm	
Texture	
Timbre / use of voices	

With the information organised this way, when you are writing a practice essay you can have the relevant pages to hand that suit just that essay, and – if the question specifies only certain elements of music – refer to those sections of each page of your revision notes.

SAMPLE ESSAY

Read the following essay as though you were an examiner. Consider the various factors listed on pages 44–45. Can you see any shortcomings? What mark out of 20 would you award this candidate?

Choose two contrasting arias from the music you have studied, and write informatively about each.

I am going to write about two arias from Handel's oratorio *Messiah*, which he wrote in 1741 for a performance in Dublin. The two arias I have chosen are 'The trumpet shall sound' and 'He was despised'.

'The trumpet shall sound' comes in part 3 of the oratorio, and is probably Handel's best-known aria for the bass voice. There is also a very important trumpet part, as suggested to Handel by the text.

There is a long introduction in which the main theme is presented on the trumpet, an immediate response to the text of the previous recitative. There are a few instances of dialogue between the trumpet and the strings. Cadences are decorated by trills in the trumpet, which gives a virtuoso touch. The bass soloist enters in bar 28. His melody is similar to the trumpet tune, and has a rising scale for 'dead shall be raised'. The very long 'A' section has a short interlude in the middle for the trumpet to give the singer a rest. It ends with a dramatic interrupted cadence and a final bar for the singer alone. The trumpet again stars in the postlude.

In the middle section, it is the trumpeter who has a rest, as the singer takes over. This middle section makes a contrast, being in B minor and having a more lyrical mood. The whole of the first section is then played again, to finish the aria in a blaze of trumpet sound.

'He was despised' is an alto aria in da capo form, with a strong contrast of mood midway. It begins in a warm E♭ major in a broad *Largo* tempo. There is a rich string tone in the first bar, but as early as bar 2 a falling three-note pattern in 3rds, suggestive of falling tears, captures a sense of sorrow. This is reinforced before the introduction is finished by some rich harmony that briefly visits a mournful E♭ minor and has several aching suspensions.

In the 'A' section the soloist's vocal line has many expressive features such as appoggiaturas on 'despised and rejected', several falling scales such as the one on 'sorrows', and the violin melody from the E♭ minor segment of the introduction for the words 'and acquainted with grief'. Perhaps most telling, as the 'A' section comes to a close, is the unaccompanied singing on 'he was despised, rejected' that conveys loneliness, and is punctuated by the tear motif. This is followed by the emotionally charged diminished 7th chord in the orchestra on 'man of sorrow', which is sustained for a bar and a half:

In the middle section, Handel portrays the scourging of Christ on Good Friday through a succession of relentless dotted rhythms in the strings. At the start of this section the key has changed to a dark C minor, and it gradually changes to G minor as the music becomes more intense. The harmony through this section is very expressive, with a number of suspensions and a powerful circle of 5ths progression midway through.

> The middle section ends dramatically: the orchestra's whipping dotted rhythms suddenly break off, and the alto soloist sings 'from shame and spitting' unaccompanied and in declamatory syllabic style that almost literally spits out the words. A simple but forthright perfect cadence ends the passage before the da capo returns the mood to the aching music of the opening section.

How well do you think the candidate has done? What are the strengths and weaknesses of the essay? Are both arias equally well treated? Has the candidate been able to 'hear' the music for both arias in the silence of the exam room? Refer to the annotated version on pages 87–89 to see how an examiner might have viewed the essay. You will find there some valuable advice for this candidate that might help you in the exam room.

FURTHER ESSAY TITLES

Here are some additional essay questions on this topic for you to try:

- What is a recitative? Explain by referring to **two** passages of recitative that you have studied, and highlight ways in which the music is expressive of the words.
- How did Baroque composers create a mood of **either** celebration **or** sadness in their music? Refer to music by **at least two** composers in your answer.
- Describe the ways in which Baroque composers have used **melody** and **texture** in their music. Refer to **at least two** pieces of music in your answer.

Area of Study 2b: Music Theatre: a study of the musical from 1940 to 1980

ORGANISING YOUR REVISION NOTES

You need to be prepared for questions that can come from three angles:

- Types of number: solo songs, ensembles, music for the chorus, music for dance

  Example: Choose two contrasting solo songs from the music you have studied, and write informatively about each.

- Different moods of music, as suggested by the lyrics or characters in the story and realised in the music

  Example: Write an essay describing how composers have used music to help to portray different characters. Refer to suitable passages from the musicals that you have studied.

- Different composers

  Example: Choose one of the following composers and write an essay that assesses his significance in the history of the musical between 1940 and 1980:

  Bernstein; Lloyd Webber; Loewe; Rodgers; Sondheim

In each case the question may steer you to talk about one or two elements of music only, such as melody, harmony and tonality, rhythm, texture, or use of voices.

*Example: Choose **two** contrasting passages from **one** musical you have studied and show how the composer has used melody and rhythm to enhance the drama.*

Bearing all these aspects in mind, you will find it helpful to organise your revision notes for this section in a methodical manner that allows for a systematic approach to learning information about different pieces that might combine to answer one of these questions.

Use a separate piece of paper for each number you have studied, and organise it in a way that will allow you to separate out all the different elements. For example:

TITLE OF NUMBER AND SHOW
Composer:
Solo / Ensemble / Chorus / Dance:
Mood:
Structure
Melody
Harmony / tonality
Rhythm
Texture
Timbre / use of voices

With the information organised this way, when you are writing a practice essay you can have the relevant pages to hand that suit just that essay, and – if the question specifies only certain elements of music – refer to those sections of each page of your revision notes.

SAMPLE ESSAY

Read the following essay as though you were an examiner. Consider the various factors listed on pages 44–45. Can you see any shortcomings? What mark out of 20 would you award this candidate?

Choose two contrasting solo songs from the music you have studied, and write informatively about each.

I am going to write about 'I could have danced all night' from My Fair Lady by Frederick Loewe, and 'Take back your mink' from Guys and Dolls by Frank Loesser.

My Fair Lady was a big hit on Broadway in 1956, and is adapted from George Bernard Shaw's play Pygmalion. The story is concerned with issues of class: Eliza, a cockney flower-girl, is trained by Professor Higgins to speak like an aristocratic girl, all because of a bet he makes with a friend (Colonel Pickering). The song comes when Eliza, at the end of a long day, finally starts to speak with the proper posh accent.

Mrs Pearce tells everyone to go to bed, and the music immediately starts up with an introductory section. The music is energetic and happy, with chirping woodwind chords. The vocal line ('Bed, bed, I couldn't go to bed') is similarly lively, with a fast tempo and short phrases.

The introduction is brief, and soon the main melody is heard. Here the vocal line is rather different: long phrases that include long notes (on 'danced', 'night' and 'more' in the opening phrase, for example) and this makes for a melody that expresses the dreamy mood that Eliza is now in. However, the chirpy and bubbly mood of the introduction is also present in the way the woodwinds accompany the singer with rapid quavers. This makes for a skilful musical portrayal of Eliza's feelings and accounts for the song's popularity. To further intensify the impact of the song, the final phrase ('I only know...') starts with a dramatic hold-back.

The main melody is repeated for a second verse, which includes some counterpoint from the maids trying to help Eliza get to bed. A third verse starts softly, but builds to a big climax, with Eliza finishing on a long sustained top G – an ending sure to inspire applause from the audience.

In 'Take back your mink' there is a slightly longer introduction. The rhythm is free – almost recitative-style – with a sense of natural speech, and pauses between each phrase. The melodic contour twists and turns in conjunct fashion, adding to the conversational flavour. Harmonically, the passage avoids any strong use of the tonic chord, which creates a sense of anticipation (where it is used, a flattened 7th is quickly introduced to move forwards to chord IV). The introduction ends with a prolonged dominant 7th.

The main refrain takes the character of an elegant Viennese waltz – conveying the sophistication of the lyrics (mink, pearls, etc.) and the romanticism of young lovers. The melodic idea is a simple two-bar shape, which is treated to a falling sequence:

5 Take back your mink, Take back your pearls.

What made you think That I was one of those girls?

The refrain follows the standard AABA song form, and the second line follows a very similar phrase, slightly adjusted at the end. For the third line, however, Loesser changes the metre to ⅜. This, coupled with a simple vocal line alternating between two notes, shows that the elegance of the waltz was just Adelaide maintaining dignity: now we realise she is in a strop! The waltz metre returns for the final 'A' phrase, and a confident perfect cadence that – finally – conclusively finds the tonic chord.

The scoring of the song is for a dance band: trumpets and saxes to the fore, and some rich bass clarinet on the bass line. There is a very telling short trumpet solo in the opening section at 'one night in his apartment' which calls for the wah-wah mute that gives a suggestive tone.

After Adelaide has sung the refrain, her 'dolls' repeat it in an upbeat ¼ version that makes the mood more defiant. A further version for dancing is played as an instrumental.

How well do you think the candidate has done? What are the strengths and weaknesses of the essay? Are both songs equally well treated? Has the candidate been able to 'hear' the music for both songs in the silence of the exam room? Refer to the annotated version on pages 89–91 to see how an examiner might have viewed the essay. You will find there some valuable advice for this candidate that might help you in the exam room.

FURTHER ESSAY TITLES

Here are some additional essay questions on this topic for you to try:

- Compare **two** passages of music from different musicals that you have studied that are intended for dance, and highlight the musical features that make them effective.
- Choose a character from any musical you have studied, and discuss how the musical features of the songs for that character create a portrayal of their personality.
- How are melody and texture used in the writing for chorus in music theatre? Refer to **at least two** different shows.

Area of Study 2c: British Popular Music from 1960 to the Present Day

ORGANISING YOUR REVISION NOTES

You need to be prepared for questions that can come from three angles:

- Historical, by decade

  Example: Choose two songs written in the 1970s, and write in detail about the musical content of each song.

- Different moods of music, as suggested by the lyrics or message of the song and realised in the music

  Example: Popular music has become increasingly used for social comment during this period. Choose two contrasting songs and write in detail about how the music is used to reflect the meaning of the words.

- By different artist or band

  Example: Choose one of the following bands and write an essay that assesses their significance in the history of British popular music since 1960:

  The Beatles; Coldplay; Duran Duran; Oasis; Pink Floyd.

In each case the question may steer you to talk about one or two elements of music only, such as melody, harmony and tonality, rhythm, texture, or the use of voices.

*Example: Choose **two** songs of contrasting mood from the 1980s and show how the artist or band has used melody and structure in their song.*

Bearing all these aspects in mind, you will find it helpful to organise your revision notes for this section in a methodical manner that allows for a systematic approach to learning information about different pieces that might combine to answer one of these questions.

Use a separate piece of paper for each song you have studied, and organise it in a way that will allow you to separate out all the different elements. For example:

TITLE OF SONG
Band / Artist: **Decade:** **Mood:**
Structure
Melody

Harmony / tonality	
Rhythm	
Texture	
Timbre / use of voices	

With the information organised this way, when you are writing a practice essay you can have the relevant pages to hand that suit just that essay, and – if the question specifies only certain elements of music – refer to those sections of each page of your revision notes.

SAMPLE ESSAY

Read the following essay as though you were an examiner. Consider the various factors listed on pages 44–45. Can you see any shortcomings? What mark out of 20 would you award this candidate?

Choose two songs written in the 1970s, and write in detail about the musical content of each song.

I am going to write about two great songs from the 70s: 'Speak To Me – Breathe' from Pink Floyd's iconic album *The Dark Side of the Moon*, and 'Somebody To Love' by the famous rock band Queen.

Pink Floyd were a London-based band who came to fame in the late 60s with their elaborate light shows. When the line-up changed in 1968, their music changed direction, and became focused on various forms of alienation such as madness and death, which appealed to those growing up in the shadow of Vietnam and the Cold War. *The Dark Side of the Moon* was released in 1973 and is the fifth highest-selling album of all time. 'Speak To Me – Breathe' is the first song on the album.

'Speak To Me' is largely not traditional music but a collage of sound effects starting with a heartbeat, created through a dampened bass drum. Other sounds heard include ticking clocks, manic laughter, a cash register and a helicopter, all sounds which were to reappear in other songs in the album. There are also fragments of conversation about madness layered on top. At the end a reversed piano chord completes the sense of build-up as the track leads immediately on into 'Breathe'.

'Breathe' has a more clearly defined beat at a slow tempo (typical of Pink Floyd) in four-time. The bass drum gives a strong downbeat to the rhythm. There is a more distinct verse structure here: eight lines that come in two halves – a change of chord sequence marking the halfway point. The same music provides an instrumental introduction with guitars and frequent slow pitch-bending. The song links into the next track on the album, 'On The Run'.

As prosperity grew in the 1970s, pop concerts increasingly were held at large stadiums such as Wembley. The song by Queen 'Somebody To Love' is representative of a style that suits such events, a style now called 'stadium rock'. The song is influenced by gospel music, especially of the style sung by Aretha Franklin. Using the latest in 1970s technology, the band members multi-tracked their voices to create the aural illusion of a 100-strong gospel choir.

The introduction to the song is sung with discreet piano backing and has a free approach to rhythm, with frequent pauses, that is typical of gospel music. The voices start on A♭ and fan out in contrary motion in a homophonic choral style.

When the first verse starts the music goes into a strict tempo (a compound four in a bar) and there is a confident, marching quality, heightened by the harmony that concentrates on major chords and keeps moving towards the sharper dominant key. This is achieved by using a B♭ major chord when the song is in A♭ major. Freddie Mercury sings the melody whilst other members of the band provide the backing vocals in a multi-tracked gospel style. The main melody tends to have a rising contour that allows for some impassioned singing at the top of the male range. Falsetto is also used at times. The 'somebody to love' line provides an infectious melodic hook, and the drumming (by Roger Taylor) makes heavy use of the crash cymbal.

There are two verses, and then a short middle section which provides a balance to the harmony of the verse by visiting the flat side: D♭ major, G♭ major, and G♭ minor. This then passes into an instrumental solo for the lead guitar (played by Brian May), which is based on the chord sequence of the verse. Voices join in at the end and lead into another vocal verse. This, however, breaks off before the refrain, and the line 'need somebody to love' is repeated many times, building from an a cappella start. A final refrain follows.

There is then a coda with several more repetitions of 'find me somebody to love', with rhythmic hand-clapping providing an infectious feature for audience participation: a significant element of stadium rock.

How well do you think the candidate has done? What are the strengths and weaknesses of the essay? Are both songs equally well treated? Has the candidate been able to 'hear' the music for both songs in the silence of the exam room? Refer to the annotated version on pages 91–93 to see how an examiner might have viewed the essay. You will find there some valuable advice for this candidate that might help you in the exam room.

FURTHER ESSAY TITLES

Here are some additional essay questions on this topic for you to try:

- What are the main differences in musical style between songs of the decade 1980–1990 and songs from the years 2000–2010? Refer to at least two songs from each period.
- What musical features make the difference between a typical ballad and a protest song?
- Choose **one** artist working in British popular music during the period, and highlight features typical of their style.

Unit 2 – Creating Musical Ideas

Content

For Unit 2 you have to write music to one of three briefs:

- Brief A: Compositional techniques
- Brief B: Free composition or pastiche in response to a given genre
- Brief C: Arranging.

Details about what exactly is required in each year are produced on the Creating Musical Ideas paper, which is available from 1 November. Your teacher will make this available to you at the point they think best fits into the course schedule that they have devised. In all, you have 20 hours of **controlled time** in which to complete one of the three briefs. Your work has to be submitted by 15 May (so you may be starting on your submission as late as April), and needs to comprise:

- A score or annotation of the music you have composed
- A recording of the piece(s) you are submitting
- The Candidate Record Form, which you must sign.

The score or annotation can be written by hand or printed from a computer. If you are answering Brief A you may write your answer on the actual question paper (but do not have to do it this way). Note that Brief A comprises two questions.

The recording may be an acoustic one of musicians performing your music, or one of the computer playback; it is an important aid to the examiner and not part of the actual assessment. The recording may be made after the 20 hours of controlled time have passed.

As this unit is more like coursework than an exam, there is no real revision required and it lies outside the main focus of this book. However, for each brief, there follows a checklist that you might use as you are getting ready to finish your work and prepare it for submission to the examiners.

> ### NOTE
>
> Note that you will not be allowed to take this book into the room where you are completing your Unit 2 work under controlled time, but you can refer to it between sessions and remind yourself of important aspects that you wish to check just before you start a controlled-time session.

Brief A – question 1

Checklist:

- Do you know what key the melody is in?
- Have you found all the modulations to related keys that occur during the melody?
- Have you finished each phrase with a suitable cadence in the right place?
- Have you used a mix of root position and first-inversion chords?
- Are all diminished chords (VII in major keys, II and VII in minor keys) in first inversion?
- Are second inversions only used in correct passing and cadential patterns?
- Have you put in all necessary accidentals when the music modulates?
- Whenever you have V^7, does the dominant 7th note fall by step on the next beat?
- Does each voice part sit in an appropriate register?
- Are the A, T and B parts easy to sing, avoiding intervals such as the augmented 4th?
- Have you found opportunity for some passing notes in lower parts?
- Do your passing notes always move by step?
- Have you checked every pair of parts to make sure there are no parallel 5ths or octaves? (Check: S/A, S/T, S/B, A/T, A/B, T/B.)

Brief A – question 2

Checklist:

- Have you chosen an appropriate tempo for your piece and provided the relevant marking at the top of the score?
- Have you indicated what instruments you are using?
- Does each melody have an essentially consonant fit with the given part, with any dissonant notes justified as passing notes, auxiliary notes or suspensions?
- Do your two melodic lines complement each other well, giving each other space in which to be heard?
- Have you made good use of the potential register for each of your chosen melodic instruments?
- Is the bass line of the given material always at the bottom of the texture throughout the piece?
- Is there a good rhythmic character to your piece?
- Do your melodic lines have a variety of conjunct and disjunct motion?
- Is there a sense of phrase structure to your melodies?
- Have you spotted and utilised any sequential passages in the given accompaniment?
- Is there a variety of textures in your piece?
- Have you made sure there are no parallel 5ths or octaves between the two melodic lines **and** between each melody and the given bass part?
- Are the melodic lines edited with appropriate phrasing, bowing, articulation and dynamic markings?

Brief B

Checklist:

- Does your piece have a clear and effective structure?
- Is there some contrast of tonality?
- Is there a good rhythmic character to your piece?
- Are the melodic ideas well shaped and memorable?
- Have you developed the melodic material and not relied solely on simple repetition?
- If your piece includes singing, does the text fit the melodic line convincingly?
- Have you created interest in your harmonic writing (for example: primary *and* secondary chords, different inversions, chromatic inflections, modulation, changing harmonic rhythm, pedal notes)?
- Is there something imaginative and varied in your handling of texture?
- Have you explored the full range of your chosen instruments in your use of register?
- Have you considered the changes of timbre that your chosen instruments offer?
- *Either:* is your score well edited with clear performance directions regarding tempo, dynamics and phrasing; *or:* does your annotation set out clearly the structure and musical content of your piece in a way that will communicate your creative ideas directly to the examiner?

Brief C

Checklist:

- Does your piece have a clear and effective structure?
- Is the majority of your piece clearly based on the given melody?
- Have you found some variety to the way you have handled the melody: for example a change of metre, a change of tonality, or a decorated version of the melody?
- Does the accompaniment to the melody have a distinct rhythmic identity?
- Have you found ways of giving the harmonic content of the arrangement interest?
- Is there something imaginative in your handling of the texture?
- Does the melody appear in a variety of registers?
- Are there ways in which your arrangement reflects the words of the folk song?
- Have you considered the changes of timbre that your chosen instruments offer?
- *Either:* is your score well edited with clear performance directions regarding tempo, dynamics and phrasing; *or:* does your annotation set out clearly the structure and musical content of your piece in a way that will communicate your creative ideas directly to the examiner?

Unit 3 - Interpreting Musical Ideas

Content

For Unit 3 you have to offer **two** of the following six options:

1. A solo performance on an instrument
2. A solo performance on voice
3. A solo performance on a second instrument
4. An ensemble performance
5. Technology option 1: sequencing
6. Technology option 2: multi-track or close-microphone recording.

Details of what is involved for each option are available in the AQA specification. You can complete your chosen two options at any point during the AS course. Your work needs to be submitted to an AQA moderator by 15 May, but needs to be marked by your teacher first, so they will give you an earlier deadline. Your submission will need to comprise:

- The recording relevant to each of your two chosen options
- Supporting material such as scores for your performances, original material for the piece you chose to sequence in option 5, and/or the initial capture of the recording you have made for option 6
- The Candidate Record Form, which you must sign, and on which your teacher will write their marks and supporting comments.

As this unit is more like coursework than an exam, there is no real revision required and it lies outside the main focus of this book. However, some checklists are provided below that you might use as you are getting ready to complete your work for this unit, so that your submission makes a favourable impression on the moderator.

Solo performances (options 1–3)

Checklist:

- Is your programme 5–8 minutes in duration?
- Is that 5–8 minutes of you playing and not relying on long introductions?
- Is that 5–8 minutes without relying on repeats of the same music played the same way?
- Are you playing the music accurately?

- Are you performing the music at the correct tempo?
- Have you given each piece a well-shaped interpretation with a good dynamic range, consideration of articulation, and appropriate use of rubato or tempo changes?
- Are you confident in the manner in which you are performing the music?
- Have you listened to the recording? If you can perform the music more accurately, or with a stronger sense of interpretation or communication, it will pay to do another take (though this will depend on how hard you have practised).
- Is the quality of the recording good?

Ensemble performance (option 4)

All the points in the checklist for solo performance apply here too. In addition:

- Does your choice of music require an ensemble of **at least three** musicians? (If your choice is only a duet, you should take advice on whether the music suits an ensemble option.)
- Is your part a unique line in the texture (i.e. not doubled by another musician)?
- Is there a tight sense of ensemble (rhythmic co-ordination) in the performance – especially at any points that the tempo changes?
- Is there a good balance of dynamic between all the musicians in the ensemble?

Sequencing (option 5)

Checklist:

- Is the original piece you have chosen to sequence **at least 32** bars long?
- Are there **at least four** independent instrumental or voice parts?
- Have you checked that a score of the original piece is being submitted with your work?
- Is one of the parts a recording of a live (acoustic) performance?
- Have you checked your sequenced version of the piece against the score for accuracy of pitch and rhythm?
- Have you made appropriate use of timbres and techniques such as panning?
- Have you considered details such as dynamics and articulation in your sequenced version?
- Does your version capture a sense of the style of the piece?
- Have you given details of the equipment you have used for your work, and the processes and decisions involved with producing your final version?

Multi-track or close-microphone recording (option 6)

Checklist:

- Is the original piece you have chosen to record **at least 32** bars long?
- Are there **at least four** independent instrumental or voice parts?
- Have you checked that a score of the original piece is being submitted with your work?
- Is the initial capture that you made of the recording included in the submission?
- Does your edited recording have a good balance and dynamic range?
- Have you made effective musical use of techniques such as reverb and delay?
- Is the quality of the recording good across a wide range of frequencies?
- Have you given details of the equipment you have used for your work, and the processes and decisions involved with producing your final edited recording?

Answers and comments on exercises for Unit 1 – Section A: Listening

EXERCISE 1

The music for the rhythm you have heard is:

ANSWERS

a. $\frac{4}{4}$
b. 8
c. Bars 1 and 2 (or bars 5 and 6)
d. Bar 3 is the rhythmic diminution of bars 1 and 2 (every note value is halved)
e. Syncopation
f. Accelerando.

COMMENTS

- The rhythm has a march-like character, typical of music in $\frac{4}{4}$ at a moderate tempo.
- Count the bars by thinking: **1**–2–3–4; **2**–2–3–4; **3**–2–3–4; **4** …
- The syncopation in bar 4 is because a half-beat is emphasised. It cannot be a hemiola, because the music is not in triple time ($\frac{3}{2}$).
- You should be able to hear the pulse getting faster towards the end.

EXERCISE 2

The music for the rhythm you have heard is:

ANSWERS

a. $\frac{3}{4}$
b. 9
c. Third
d. Dotted rhythm

e. Triplet rhythm

f. Hemiola.

COMMENTS

■ The rhythm has a gentle lilting quality that is common of music in triple time.

■ Count the bars carefully! There is one more than you might reasonably guess...

■ Careful listening is required to hear that the music starts with an upbeat. It is difficult to realise on first listening, but as the opening becomes more familiar on subsequent hearings, it should be clear that the second beat you hear is more stressed than the first.

■ The hemiola should be clear to hear. From bar 5 try counting like this: **1**–2–3; **1**–2–3; **1**–and–2–and–3–and; **1**.

■ There is a very distinctive kick in the rhythm that is only possible in triple time.

EXERCISE 3

The music for the rhythm you have heard is:

ANSWERS

a. $\frac{6}{8}$

b. 2

c. 1

d. Quaver

e. Bar 7

f. Ritenuto.

COMMENTS

■ You should feel quite clearly that there are only two beats in each bar. If in doubt, think like a soldier marching: 'left, right, left, right'.

■ However, each beat subdivides into three, which makes for a compound time signature. Think: **1**–and–a–2–and–a; **1**–and–a–2–and–a; **1** ...

■ This means that the 'beat' is a dotted crotchet, so that the subdivision can be represented by three quavers (which, of course, makes one-and-a-half crotchets).

■ Therefore the first – unaccented – note at the start is just a quaver.

■ You should be able to hear the pulse getting slower towards the end.

EXERCISE 4

The music for the rhythm you have heard is:

ANSWERS

a. Additive
b. 4
c. It is longer than beats 1, 2 and 3 (being worth a dotted crotchet)
d. 8
e. The 4th beat now has a dotted rhythm pattern.

COMMENTS

■ The slightly lopsided 'limp' to the rhythm here is due to the additive rhythm.
■ The four beats per bar are three crotchets and one dotted crotchet.

EXERCISE 5

The music for the melody you have heard is:

ANSWERS

a. Major
b. Conjunct and diatonic
c. Conjunct
d. Triadic
e. It is chromatic
f. Bars 1–4: both phrases are conjunct

g. A turn at the end of bars 2 and 6.

COMMENTS

- The melody has that bright, sunny mood of a major key which is evident from the third note.
- The music in bars 1–4 is diatonic because there are no sharps or flats; there are no leaps in contour, so the melody is conjunct; scalic is not so appropriate since it twists and changes direction several times (unlike a scale).
- In bars 5–6 none of the notes are neighbours, so you might think disjunct was a good description; however, all the notes here (Cs, Es and Gs) belong to a tonic chord of C major, so triadic is a much more precise description.
- The sharps and flats in bars 7–8 make the music chromatic (rather than diatonic), but there are no leaps here, so it is once again conjunct.

EXERCISE 6

The music for the melody you have heard is:

ANSWERS

a. Minor
b. Scalic
c. Bars 1 and 2: descending; bars 3 and 4: ascending; bars 5 and 6: descending
d. It becomes disjunct
e. A trill
f. An octave.

COMMENTS

- The melody hints at a minor key almost immediately due to the fall of a tone from the first note (which is, as in many tunes, the tonic). Were it in a major key, the leading note would be a semitone below the tonic. The G♯ in bar 3 confirms the key.
- The falling scales in bars 1 and 2 take the form of descending melodic minor scales (with F♮ and G♮).
- The rising scales in bars 3 and 4 follow an ascending melodic scale (with F♯ and G♯).
- Bars 7 and 8 comprise a series of wide leaps, creating a distinctly disjunct outline.

EXERCISE 7

The music for the melody you have heard is:

ANSWERS

a. 6
b. It is a sequence of the first phrase, at a lower pitch
c. It is the inversion of the first half of the melody
d. A pentatonic scale.

COMMENTS

- The melody is clearly structured with six two-bar phrases.
- You need to listen carefully to hear the inversion in the second half of the melody.
- The pentatonic character is audible with a mix of tones and minor 3rds in the melodic line.

EXERCISE 8

The music for the melody you have heard is:

ANSWERS

a. Use of blue notes; syncopation
b. A glissando
c. It becomes scalic; it uses a whole-tone scale; it is played staccato
d. Pizzicato.

COMMENTS

- The melody is, essentially, in a major key: as confirmed by the E♮ in bar 2. but the E♭s in bar 1 immediately give a 'blues' sound. The G♭ and E♭ in bar 3, and B♭ at the end are also 'blue notes'.
- The glissando in bar 4 is played on the violin by sliding a finger down the string whilst bowing.
- The whole-tone scale makes for a very haunting effect; every interval is a tone.

EXERCISE 9

Here are the eight different versions of the missing bar 3:

COMMENTS

In (a) you should have heard that the first missing note is the same as the last given note. The melody then falls stepwise and the link to the final note is the standard leading note-to-tonic semitone step.

In versions (b) to (d) you can hear that the first missing note is a step down from the last given note. Each then has its own contour. In (b) you should hear that the last missing note is the same as the note in bar 4. In (c) listen carefully for the last missing note: it is just a step above the tonic in bar 4, and this creates a small jump (of a 3rd) in the contour of bar 3. In (d) there is a leap either side of the last note in bar 3, and it is important to realise that the melody ends dominant to tonic: a sound that you should be able to recognise confidently (think of the first two notes of 'O Little Town of Bethlehem', or the opening notes of Mozart's *Eine kleine Nachtmusik*).

There is a catch in (e): the first missing note is lower than the last given note, but not by step. Instead it starts on the tonic – a note you have heard three times in the first six notes of the melody. The contour of the missing bar here is all conjunct.

In versions (f) to (h) the first missing note is a step up from the last given note. There are some leaps to work out in these versions, which makes it important to think about the link to the note in bar 4. In (f) and (h) this is the standard leading note-to-tonic semitone, but in (g) it is a falling octave – an interval that is fairly clear to hear. The E♭ in (h) is a tricky note to identify: you should be able to hear that it is higher than the previous note, but it has a distinct colour (almost a 'blue' note). Remember 'chromatic' means 'colour': the E♭ makes it distinctly different to the version in (f).

EXERCISE 10

Here is the music you have just heard:

ANSWERS

a. Major
b. An upper auxiliary note
c. An imperfect cadence
d. A passing note
e. A perfect cadence: Ic–V–I
f. No. It ends in the dominant.

COMMENTS

- The music has a confident, bright character, and is clearly in a major key.
- Both decorative notes are in the melody and should be clear to hear at the slow tempo.
- The first cadence ends on a different chord from the opening tonic chord; however, the music is not left hanging in mid-air as with an interrupted cadence. It is therefore an imperfect cadence. This one is Ic–V, otherwise known as a half-close.

- The final cadence is much more commanding and clearly a perfect cadence. The same note is in the bass for both chords that precede the final tonic chord: a common occurrence and a certain clue to a Ic–V–I cadence.
- If you don't spot it on first listening, you can hear when the second playing starts that the music ended in a different key from where it began. The move to the dominant is achieved through an extra sharp (in this case C♯), which makes the music sound brighter when it first appears.

EXERCISE 11

Here is the music you have just heard:

ANSWERS

a. Minor
b. A pedal note
c. Second time it is a dominant pedal; at the start it was a tonic pedal
d. Yes
e. A plagal cadence (IV–I)
f. A tierce de Picardie.

COMMENTS

- From the very start the music has the dark character of a minor key.
- The pedal notes are reiterated in between each chord to make them clearer to hear.
- You should be able to hear the same tonic chord starting the second listening as was present at the end of the first hearing.
- The tonic note is present in the penultimate chord as well as the final chord: a good way to test for a plagal cadence. (In a perfect cadence the leading note is in the penultimate chord, and the tonic would clash with this if you try singing it at the same time.)
- Although the tonic is the same at the end as at the beginning, the final chord has a bright major third: the hallmark of a tierce de Picardie.

EXERCISE 12

Here is the music you have just heard:

ANSWERS

a. Dissonant
b. A circle of 5ths progression
c. An interrupted cadence (Ic–V–VI)
d. A minor: the relative minor
e. A perfect cadence (Ic–V⁷–I).

COMMENTS

- The first chord is an abrasive, clashing combination of notes and not related to the key suggested by the opening arpeggio. It is therefore dissonant.
- Listen carefully for the note in the bass on the downbeat of each bar to hear the circle of 5ths. This always produces a descending sequence in the harmony. Sometimes, though not on this occasion, the melody will follow suit and also have a sequence when the circle of 5ths is used in the harmony.
- Despite the silence, the cadence at the end of the flowing melody leaves an open-ended feel, and one senses more music is needed: a sure sign of an interrupted cadence.
- The rather surprise ending takes the music to the relative minor. Try playing the piece with the following three bars instead to stay in C major:

EXERCISE 13

Here is the music you have just heard:

ANSWERS

a. Modal
b. It is an appoggiatura
c. The harmonic rhythm is much faster (every beat rather than one chord per bar)
d. There is a suspension.

COMMENTS

■ The piece has a sense of a minor mood, but the leading note is never sharpened, and this means that chord V is never heard as a major triad (e.g. bars 4 and 8). The result means that the piece has the plaintive feel of music in a minor mode (in this case the Aeolian mode).

- There is a blatant clash on the first downbeat between the note in the melody and the note in the bass. The chord fills in and the melody resolves to a harmony note. Given that the melody note on the downbeat was approached by leap from the anacrusis, this makes it an appoggiatura. Several others can be heard in the piece.
- Contrast in music can be provided in many ways; here the middle phrase gains much of its different character from the quicker harmonic rhythm, one of the more subtle but telling ways of achieving contrast.
- The suspension on the last chord is found in the middle of the chord; the D from the previous chord is reiterated as the 4th in the tonic chord and finally resolves to the 3rd.

EXERCISE 14

Here is the music you have just heard:

ANSWERS AND COMMENTS ON EXERCISES FOR UNIT 1 – SECTION A: LISTENING

ANSWERS

a. Melody with accompaniment
b. The melody is heard in the bass (or left hand of the piano)
c. Major 6th
d. A turn
e. Interrupted cadence
f. Plagal cadence.

COMMENTS

- There is a clear, single melodic line which is accompanied by a chordal figuration (known as an Alberti bass).
- For the second phrase the texture inverts: the melody is played in a lower register.
- The upbeat is the dominant note, but this rises to the third and not the tonic (in much the same way that 'My Bonnie Lies Over the Ocean' starts).
- The piece could end after the third phrase if the Ic–V progression in bar 11 resolved onto chord I for a perfect cadence in bar 12, but this is sidestepped to make an interrupted cadence.
- The penultimate chord has the tonic in the melody – a strong clue to this being a plagal ending.

EXERCISE 15

Here is the music you have just heard:

ANSWERS

a. Contrapuntal
b. Minor
c. The opening music returns but the texture is inverted – that is, the original upper melody is now in the bass
d. Perfect cadence
e. Trill
f. Inverted mordent.

COMMENTS

■ There are two strands to the texture, and both have a strong melodic character with independent rhythms and contours. This makes the music strongly contrapuntal.

■ The minor flavour is apparent from the very beginning: there is a minor 3rd on the downbeat and immediately the tonic in the bass is decorated with the sharpened leading note.

■ Fix the opening to the upper line in your memory – an A minor broken chord in crotchets, and listen for this shape in the bass when the music turns f. Meanwhile, what was the bass at the start – a conjunct shape built from a rising A minor scale – is now in the upper line at this point.

EXERCISE 16

Here is the music you have just heard:

ANSWERS

a. Canonic
b. Major
c. C major
d. $\frac{3}{4}$
e. Hemiola
f. Perfect cadence.

COMMENTS

- Throughout the piece the bass line copies the melody, starting one bar later and one octave lower.
- The melody is largely conjunct and, but for a few accidentals, outlines an F major scale fairly clearly.
- The appearance of B♮s from bar 12 makes the music sound brighter and lifts the piece into its dominant key of C major.
- The music has the lilting feel of triple time, though at this speed you might count one in a bar.
- The hemiola is a little hidden, but the combined accentuation between the two hands highlights, from bar 12: **1**–2–3; **1**–2–3; **1**–and–2–and–3–and; **1**.

EXERCISE 17

Here is the music you have just heard:

ANSWERS

a. Homophonic
b. $\frac{6}{8}$ – compound time
c. Syncopation
d. Sequence
e. F minor
f. Tierce de Picardie.

COMMENTS

- Throughout, the musical substance is the chord progression; the melodic line is formed by the top note of each chord: a classic homophonic texture.
- Each beat has a long + short subdivision (or 'tum-ti-tum', if you prefer): typical of compound time. There are two beats in each bar.
- The *sfz* moment in bar 4 does not occur on one of the main beats and thus forms a syncopation.
- The sequential pattern falls through three bars.
- The music modulates to the relative minor in the second half.
- The final chord, in a phrase in F minor, is F major. This is a tierce de Picardie and not a late modulation to F major (which is a distant key from the original tonic of A♭ major).

EXERCISE 18

Here is the music you have just heard:

ANSWERS

a. Fugal
b. Seven times
c. It is played at half speed (rhythmic diminution) and in octaves
d. Major (though it passes through a minor key in the middle)
e. Perfect cadence
f. A suspension – actually three of them!

COMMENTS

■ This piece is contrapuntal: three independent melodic lines. However, there is a regularly recurring melodic theme that is heard at the start and returns in each part at different pitches. This makes the texture fugal. In all, the theme is played seven times.

■ The final entry of the fugue subject is given extra weight by being played in octaves in the bass, and with rhythmic diminution.

Here is the music you have just heard:

ANSWERS

a. Homophonic and antiphonal
b. Circle of 5ths
c. The leading legato phrase is now in the bass register and the answering staccato phrase is now in the treble register.

COMMENTS

The music is clearly chordal in nature, and the texture can therefore be called homophonic. In addition, phrases (and later just individual chords) alternate between treble and bass registers, giving an antiphonal effect to the texture as well.

EXERCISE 20

The instrumentation of the figures is:

1st time	French horn
2nd time	French horn
3rd time	French horn
4th time	Clarinet
5th time	Clarinet
6th time	Cor anglais
7th time	French horn
8th time	Cor anglais
9th time	Flute
10th time	Cor anglais
11th time	Flute

Answers and comments on specimen questions for Unit 1 – Section A: Listening

QUESTION 1

ANSWERS

a. Viola
b. Turn
c. Clarinet
d. Ascending chromatic (1 mark for each word)
e. Major
f. Dominant
g. Melody with accompaniment
h. Perfect
i. $\frac{6}{8}$.

COMMENTS

a. A tricky question – were you tempted to put violin or cello? The viola has a distinctive timbre in between the two – it is well worth being sure you know the difference.
b. It is possible to do this question by elimination, though you should recognise the graceful flurry of notes created by a turn.
c. Hopefully an easy mark here…
d. Did you only write one word? There were two marks…
e. Another easy mark.
f. Could you hear the brighter key at this point? If not did you *think*? This is a Classical-style piece in a major key: second themes in such music are nearly always in the dominant.
g. This is a very good example of melody with accompaniment.
h. A perfect cadence is what you would expect at the end of a musical paragraph in the Classical style.
i. You should have felt the two beats in a bar, but did you spot each beat was subdivided into three to create compound time?

QUESTION 2

ANSWERS

a. Timpani
b. 5th
c.

d. Piccolo and glockenspiel

e. The melody is played in octaves

f. Modal.

COMMENTS

a. The timpani are playing with the bass line.

b. The chords are Dm^9 and Gm^9 with the G a perfect 5th below the D.

c. You should have heard that the first of the missing notes is the same as the last given note in this question; the shape is mostly conjunct and the lead back to the E printed in the question is from a step underneath.

d. If you thought flute, listen again to the piccolo starting the fugue in Britten's *Young Person's Guide to the Orchestra* and compare it with this piece. The glockenspiel – the most common mallet instrument in the orchestra – comprises metal bars and gives the tinkling sparkle clearly audible here.

e. Listen carefully if you missed this: the cellos are playing the melody as well, at a lower octave than the violins.

f. There are no sharpened leading notes here at all, giving a very pastoral, folk quality that is typical of modal music.

QUESTION 3

ANSWERS

a. Violin

b. Arco

c.

d. Diatonic

e. Canonic

f. Perfect

g. The music ends in the same key as it began.

COMMENTS

a. An easy mark, hopefully.

b. Again, should be easy, so long as you know your string playing terminology.

c. The clues you need to spot here are: 1) the first missing note is lower than both of the first two notes that are given; 2) the contour is stepwise and descending; 3) the final note on the downbeat is the same as the next downbeat. It also helps if you realise the first note is the tonic.

d. All being well you have just completed the notation for the first phrase. There are no accidentals; there are more than five pitches used: it is diatonic.

e. Did you spot this? Listen carefully to the piano: it is a bar ahead of the violin, playing the identical melody throughout the excerpt (one octave lower).

f. A conclusive cadence, in which you cannot hear the tonic in the penultimate chord: it therefore has to be perfect.

g. You should be able to hear that the music resumes in the same key as it finishes when you hear subsequent playings. However, around 0:20 it has temporarily moved to the relative minor, so the first of the possible answers cannot be true.

QUESTION 4

ANSWERS

a. Oboe
b. Pizzicato
c. Minor
d. Cellos
e. A rising scale in octaves
f. Flute
g. Circle of 5ths harmony; imperfect cadence; sequence *(1 mark for each)*
h. $\frac{2}{4}$.

COMMENTS

a. No instrument does poignant loneliness as well as a solo oboe; this is a fine example.
b. An easy mark, hopefully.
c. The dark, plaintive mood of this piece is largely due to its minor tonality.
d. The rich tenor register of the cello is a great timbre for an expressive melody such as this one.
e. Hopefully you heard the rising scale, but did you notice that the clarinets are in octaves? Listen carefully…
f. Flutes are usually considered to be high-pitched instruments, but they have a rich, warm tone in their lowest octave, as heard here.
g. Most of the cadences in this passage (at the end of each melodic phrase) are imperfect. (Perfect cadences mark the end of the melody, both in the oboe and cellos.) The melodic sequence and circle of 5ths harmony occur simultaneously, as is often the case.

QUESTION 5

ANSWERS

a. There is a **two**-part texture doubled at **three** different octaves
b. Sequence
c. C major (the dominant)
d. Pedal note
e. Horns and then bassoons
f. 3rd
g. Bar 35 beat 1 or 3
h. Binary.

COMMENTS

a. Central to getting this correct is to remember about transposing instruments. When the title for an instrument includes a note, for example 'in B♭', you must remember that a written C will sound that note. Here we have 'Horns in F' and the first note for the second horn is a *written* C, so that will *sound* F – the F at the octave between the second oboe and the second bassoon. The conclusion is that for this whole phrase these six instruments are providing two lines, each doubled at three octaves. If in doubt: listen.

b. The sequence is straightforward to hear and see, both in the melody and the harmony.

c. The most likely modulation (by far) in the Classical style.

d. The pedal note is played (as reiterated crotchets) by cellos and violas in unison. Given the music has already modulated by this point it is actually a tonic pedal, though only one mark is available so 'pedal' is enough.

e. Again, you have to remember about the transposing horns here... or just listen carefully. The '2 marks' indication shows that two different instruments are required here.

f. Here you need to be sure about reading the alto clef in the viola part. The middle line of the stave is middle C.

g. This kind of a question takes patient and methodical searching. Make sure you give both bar *and* beat number if that is what is required. If you only write the bar number you will not get the mark.

h. Two halves, both repeating and modulating to the dominant at the halfway point make up classic binary form.

QUESTION 6

ANSWERS

a. A turn

b. Ic *or* tonic second inversion

c. V^7 *or* dominant 7th root position

d. C minor

e. Circle of 5ths

f. A trill

g. An octave

h. Bar 16 *or* 17.

COMMENTS

a. The turns are not shown in the score, but listen carefully...

b. Note there are two marks available: you need to earn both! This is the start of a classic Ic–V^7–I perfect cadence...

c. ... which continues here.

d. Don't fall into the trap of seeing a key signature and giving the associated major key. Listen: Reicha has gone into the tonic minor.

e. You should be able to hear this, but you can certainly see it in the bass line (played, appropriately enough, by the bassoon).

f. This is easier to hear than the oboe turn: it lasts longer.

g. You have to remember that the clarinet in B♭ is a transposing instrument. Or just use your ears...

h. Again, remember the horn in F is a transposing instrument (sounding a 5th lower: written C sounds F). Then search methodically.

Comments on sample essays for Unit 1 – Section B: Historical Study

Here is an annotated version of the sample essay on page 39 of the revision guide.

Write an informative account of the introduction in the first movement of this symphony. You should refer to structure, melody, texture, instrumentation, rhythm, harmony and tonality.

Haydn was born in Austria in 1732. He spent most of his career working for a Prince at Esterhazy, but wrote his final symphony for the London concert scene in 1795 when Salomon invited the great composer to visit Britain. The symphony is written for a large Classical orchestra with a full range of wind instruments as well as trumpets and timpani.[1]

Haydn starts the symphony with a slow introduction, something he had done in many of his previous 103 symphonies.[2] The symphony begins with the full orchestra playing *forte* for two bars, including some exciting drum rolls on the timpani.[3] All instruments are playing the same tune in different octaves.[4] This tune has a strong dotted rhythm pattern.[5] This makes a stirring start to the piece and makes a very grand effect.[6]

The following four bars by contrast are *piano* and mysterious.[7] A solo bassoon is supported by the lower strings[8] and the first violins answer in the second half of each bar. This section ends with a perfect cadence in bar 6,[9] which is followed by a repeat of the opening two bars, returning to **ff**, but now at a different pitch.[10]

Haydn then returns to the *piano* idea from bar 3, only this time lengthens the phrase to five bars with the inclusion of a solo flute. Also, this time the passage

---

1 This opening paragraph gives accurate context, but is of limited value in addressing the question.
2 This contextual comment is more relevant to the question.
3 True, but the analysis is starting with detail about the first two bars; we do not have any sense of an overview of the introduction.
4 It would be beneficial to comment more specifically about this 'tune': the fact that it is built from just two notes of the scale – the tonic and dominant – and therefore announces the key note of the symphony (D), although keeps open the issue of whether it is major or minor.
5 Not just dotted, but double dotted.
6 A useful comment about how these first two bars actually sound. Other useful words could be formal, solemn and declamatory.
7 This is a reasonable description, but in what follows there is little explanation of what accounts for the sense of mystery: the music being in D minor (when the symphony is actually going to be in D major!), the conjunct melodic shape (in contrast to the leaps of bars 1–2), the hint of chromaticism, and the non-root position harmony.
8 This is a confused comment: the bassoon is not a significant solo line, but doubling the violas in order to enrich the sonority of the texture. There is a suspicion now that the candidate has not accurately heard the music when reading the score in the silence of the exam room.
9 Somewhat imprecise: the perfect cadence comes on to the downbeat of bar 7.
10 It is important to note the change of key here (to F major, the relative major). Also, the candidate has not commented on the fact that the brass and timpani do not play this time.

begins with a rising sequence as bar 5 is repeated up a tone in the next bar[11] in order to add interest.[12]

There is one more appearance of the opening ff idea at bar 14, only this time there is a surprise as the second bar is suddenly pp and played by the strings only.[13] The introduction ends with a Ic to V[7] cadence.[14] This leaves a sense of suspense which gets resolved when the Allegro starts.[15]

Here is an annotated version of the sample essay on page 42 of the revision guide.

Describe the ways in which Haydn makes use of rhythm in the third movement of this symphony.

Haydn writes a traditional minuet for the third movement, and indicates that this should be played in a lively manner ('Allegro'). By choosing a time signature of ¾[16] Haydn ensures that the music will have a dance character.[17] Also the music is in D major and begins forte so there is a confident and positive start.[18] The opening plays the same phrase twice, but Haydn shows that the music should be played piano second time.[19]

From bar 17 the tune is in crotchets for some time and then the music runs down the scale in quavers for extra energy.[20] The music here is quite chromatic[21] which gives a sense of being the middle of the minuet. For instance, the B♭s from bar 30 mean the music is in F major here.[22] The music then returns to the opening tune.[23] There is a strange break for two bars towards the end of the minuet.[24]

---

11   This is a correct and good observation, but there is more to say here about the chromatic element to these five bars, especially in bar 12. There is no explanation that the music is coming back to D minor.
12   'To add interest' is a top examiner wincing moment! It does not show musical understanding. Avoid it.
13   This is a good observation, but the candidate has overlooked the fact that Haydn now goes from D to G (the subdominant) and then harmonises this on the last beat with the colourful Neapolitan chord (E♭ major), which helps to suggest that something momentous is about to happen (i.e. the Allegro is about to start).
14   Good, but it would be better to give the bar and beat numbers.
15   True. It would be good to point out that D minor is about to give way to D major.
16   Minuets by definition are in triple time so Haydn is not making the choice at this point.
17   It isn't just the metre that creates the dance feel, but the articulation: staccato first and second beats, and *sf* third beats that are slurred on to the next downbeat. It is also the case that this rhythmic character is clear throughout the homophonic texture. The anacrusis helps, too.
18   A true sentence, but not really relevant to a question about rhythm.
19   Again, this is not about rhythm.
20   This is true for the melody, but there is a significant rhythmic feature in the bass (replicated in the woodwinds) that is missed: in bars 21–24 there is a hemiola cross-rhythm in the bass line.
21   The candidate has again wandered off the question. Chromaticism cannot relate to rhythm.
22   This is not only irrelevant to the question, but inaccurate too. With C♯s still in the first violins, these B♭s are suggesting D minor, not F major. It would seem that the candidate has stopped imagining the sound of the music when writing this sentence.
23   Yes, but the melodic line is decorated with further quavers, making the music more lively here rather than the very formal (even aristocratic) crotchets at the start of the minuet.
24   'Strange' does not give the best insight here. It is a tremendously effective breaking off of the music which then resumes via the long (two-bar) trill; this relates back to bar 7 of the main theme for the movement – a trill for most of the orchestra on a dotted minim – which is something that the candidate did not mention earlier.

The trio section continues in the same tempo and time signature.[25] There are far more quavers here to create a greater sense of excitement in the music,[26] but also more dotted minims too, as in the flute part at bar 84.[27] The brass and timpani do not play in the trio because it is in a different key.[28] Haydn provides an additional section at the end of the trio to lead back to the minuet which stands out because it does not have any quavers.

---

25 True, but the candidate has not picked up on the anacrusis crotchet-minim pattern that comes twice at the start of the trio, and is rather more graceful than the somewhat stomping crotchets at the start of the minuet.

26 If you listen to the music, these legato quavers are bringing elegance, not excitement, to the music here. It would be worth mentioning the simple triple-time rhythm of the pizzicato chords underneath, which – due to the clever use of rests – keeps the listener aware of the triple-time metre under the long line of even notes in the melody.

27 This is a valid point, but the significant use of the crotchet-minim pattern from bar 65 has not been commented upon.

28 True, but the examiner cannot give credit to this point in an essay that is answering a question about rhythm.

Comments on sample essays for Unit 1 – Section C: Historical Study

Here is an annotated version of the essay on Baroque Choral Music on pages 46–48 of the revision guide.

Choose two contrasting arias from the music you have studied, and write informatively about each.

I am going to write about two arias from Handel's oratorio Messiah, which he wrote in 1741 for a performance in Dublin. The two arias I have chosen are 'The trumpet shall sound' and 'He was despised'.[1]

'The trumpet shall sound' comes in part 3 of the oratorio, and is probably Handel's best-known aria for the bass voice.[2] There is also a very important trumpet part,[3] as suggested to Handel by the text.

There is a long introduction in which the main theme[4] is presented on the trumpet, an immediate response to the text of the previous recitative.[5] There are a few instances of dialogue between the trumpet and the strings.[6] Cadences are decorated by trills in the trumpet, which gives a virtuoso touch.[7] The bass soloist enters in bar 28.[8] His melody is similar to the trumpet tune, and has a rising scale for 'dead shall be raised'. The very long 'A' section has a short interlude in the middle for the trumpet to give the singer a rest.[9] It ends with a dramatic interrupted cadence and a final bar for the singer alone.[10] The trumpet again stars in the postlude.[11]

---

1 Candidates are often tempted to spend time writing about what they are going to write about, but it is just a waste of precious time in the exam room and will not gain any marks. Much better just to start writing about the music. The facts there – year and place – may give a touch of context, but are not very relevant to the question.
2 Again, this sentence has limited benefit.
3 A chance has been missed here to use technical vocabulary: obbligato.
4 Some detail about this trumpet melody would help – the rising arpeggio and dotted rhythms at the start, the conjunct even quavers in the upper register, and so on.
5 Good awareness of the context of the aria in the overall story of the whole piece.
6 More detail about this would be beneficial.
7 True, though a more telling, stylistic point would be to mention that there are hemiolas at the cadences (the aria being in triple time – which is not mentioned here).
8 There is not a lot to be gained from knowing the bar number here: it is a waste of memory. The musical description of the moment is 'the first entry of the bass' and not 'bar 28'; the latter you might muddle up and get wrong, the former is very easy to remember, and very precise.
9 It is true that there is an interlude, but its significance is missed: it articulates the structure of the 'A' section, by occurring when the music has reached a halfway point of cadencing in A major – the dominant. Also, the candidate has referred to 'A' section at this point without first mentioning that the aria is in da capo (or ternary) form.
10 True, although not very clear: the key is not mentioned; neither is the final perfect cadence after the dramatic interrupted cadence.
11 A somewhat informal description. The codetta (not postlude) balances the introduction.

In the middle section, it is the trumpeter who has a rest,[12] as the singer takes over. This middle section makes a contrast, being in B minor[13] and having a more lyrical mood.[14] The whole of the first section is then played again, to finish the aria in a blaze of trumpet sound.

'He was despised' is an alto aria in da capo form,[15] with a strong contrast of mood midway. It begins in a warm Eb major in a broad Largo tempo. There is a rich string tone in the first bar, but as early as bar 2[16] a falling three-note pattern in thirds, suggestive of falling tears, captures a sense of sorrow. This is reinforced before the introduction is finished by some rich harmony that briefly visits a mournful Eb minor and has several aching suspensions.[17]

In the 'A' section the soloist's vocal line has many expressive features such as appoggiaturas on 'despised and rejected', several falling scales such as the one on 'sorrows', and the violin melody from the Eb minor segment of the introduction for the words 'and acquainted with grief'. Perhaps most telling, as the 'A' section comes to a close, is the unaccompanied singing on 'he was despised, rejected' that conveys loneliness, and is punctuated by the tear motif. This is followed by the emotionally charged diminished seventh chord in the orchestra on 'man of sorrow',[18] which is sustained for a bar and a half:[19]

In the middle section, Handel portrays the scourging of Christ on Good Friday[20] through a succession of relentless dotted rhythms in the strings. At the start

---

12 Actually the orchestra is tacet too: the middle section is accompanied only by the continuo instruments.
13 Yes, the middle section starts in B minor, but it modulates to F# minor by the end.
14 It would be good to know what musical features makes the middle section more lyrical: an absence of dotted rhythms, long conjunct melismas, sequential patterns, and so on.
15 A clear statement of structure at the start makes further references to structure simple and clear to make in due course.
16 This isn't a feat of bar number memory: it's very easy to remember what happens in the second bar.
17 Lots of good detail about the introduction – instrumentation, melodic shape, harmonic colour – all in an efficient manner.
18 Again, plenty of varied detail, chosen from across the 'A' section. Location has been defined through the relevant words of the text – a much easier way to recall the detail than bar numbers, so long as you can 'hear' the music going through your mind in the exam room. This is why playing and singing it are very valuable ways of revising, not just listening to it. Interact with your music!
19 Quoting the melody and accompaniment for this passage – accurately – is impressive, and supports the analytical comment in an efficient way.
20 Clear awareness of the context of this movement in the story of the oratorio as a whole.

of this section the key has changed to a dark C minor, and it gradually changes to G minor as the music becomes more intense.[21] The harmony through this section is very expressive, with a number of suspensions and a powerful circle of 5ths progression midway through.[22]

The middle section ends dramatically: the orchestra's whipping dotted rhythms suddenly break off, and the alto soloist sings 'from shame and spitting' unaccompanied and in declamatory syllabic style that almost literally spits out the words.[23] A simple but forthright perfect cadence ends the passage before the da capo returns the mood to the aching music of the opening section.[24]

Here is an annotated version of the essay on music theatre on pages 50–51 of the revision guide.

Choose two contrasting solo songs from the music you have studied, and write informatively about each.

I am going to write about 'I could have danced all night' from My Fair Lady by Frederick Loewe, and 'Take back your mink' from Guys and Dolls by Frank Loesser.[25]

My Fair Lady was a big hit on Broadway in 1956, and is adapted from George Bernard Shaw's play Pygmalion. The story is concerned with issues of class: Eliza, a cockney flower-girl, is trained by Professor Higgins to speak like an aristocratic girl, all because of a bet he makes with a friend (Colonel Pickering). The song comes when Eliza, at the end of a long day, finally starts to speak with the proper posh accent.[26] Mrs Pearce tells everyone to go to bed, and the music immediately starts up with an introductory section. The music is energetic and happy, with chirping woodwind chords.[27] The vocal line ('Bed, bed, I couldn't go to bed') is similarly lively, with a fast tempo and short phrases.[28]

The introduction is brief, and soon the main melody is heard. Here the vocal line is rather different: long phrases that include long notes (on 'danced', 'night' and 'more' in the opening phrase, for example) and this makes for a melody that expresses the dreamy mood that Eliza is now in.[29] However, the chirpy and bubbly mood of the

---

21 Accurate knowledge of the structure of the music, **and** awareness of the effect of that structure on the emotional content of the music.

22 Good detail of the harmonic language here. Do you think the candidate learned this, or did they have the music running through their mind when writing the essay?

23 Excellent description of the music and its expressive impact.

24 A good rounding off of the second half of the essay.

25 Candidates are often tempted to spend time writing about what they are going to write about, but it is just a waste of precious time in the exam room and will not gain any marks. Much better just to start writing about the music.

26 Write about the music! This paragraph giving a context for the song can be greatly reduced.

27 These chords could be usefully analysed: they are not just standard triads.

28 The introduction is rather glossed over: there is a structure to it (in two halves) that would bear discussion.

29 A reasonable description of the melody, though the rising arpeggio anacrusis (that throws emphasis onto 'danced') might be mention – after all, it comes twice in the phrase.

introduction is also present in the way the woodwinds accompany the singer with rapid quavers.[30] This makes for a skilful musical portrayal of Eliza's feelings and accounts for the song's popularity. To further intensify the impact of the song, the final phrase ('I only know...') starts with a dramatic hold-back.[31]

The main melody is repeated for a second verse, which includes some counterpoint[32] from the maids trying to help Eliza get to bed.[33] A third verse starts softly, but builds to a big climax, with Eliza finishing on a long sustained top G – an ending sure to inspire applause from the audience.[34]

In 'Take back your mink' there is a slightly longer introduction.[35] Here Adelaide is reminiscing about her relationship with Nathan, and all the gifts he showered upon her. This is captured in the freedom of the rhythm – almost recitative-style[36] – with a sense of natural speech, and pauses between each recollection. The melodic contour twists and turns in conjunct fashion, adding to the conversational flavour.[37] Harmonically, the passage avoids any strong use of the tonic chord, which creates a sense of anticipation (where it is used, a flattened 7th is quickly introduced to move forwards to chord IV). The introduction ends with a prolonged dominant 7th.[38]

The main refrain takes the character of an elegant Viennese waltz – conveying the sophistication of the lyrics (mink, pearls, etc.) and the romanticism of young lovers.[39] The melodic idea is a simple two-bar shape, which is treated to a falling sequence:[40]

---

30   Good awareness of the orchestration in the accompaniment, though the doubling of vocal melody in various octaves on the strings is another important factor that does not get mentioned here.

31   The structure of this refrain is overlooked. It is essentially in 32-bar song form (AABA), but – interestingly – the second phrase is not a direct repeat of the first, staring a tone higher and suggesting sequence. Has the candidate 'heard' the music in the exam room?

32   Good use of technical vocabulary…

33   …but more detail needed to describe the clever juxtaposition of moods and motifs here.

34   There is little different in the final verse, but mention of the harmony and orchestration at the end could be made perhaps.

35   In writing about this song, the candidate gets to the music straight away.

36   Good vocabulary.

37   A good, efficient description.

38   Excellent awareness of the harmonic writing.

39   Good comment and awareness of context.

40   Quoting the opening eight-bar phrase – accurately – is impressive, and supports the analytical comment in an efficient way.

The refrain follows the standard AABA song form,[41] and the second line follows a very similar phrase, slightly adjusted at the end. For the third line, however, Loesser changes the metre to $\frac{3}{4}$. This, coupled with a simple vocal line alternating between two notes, shows that the elegance of the waltz was just Adelaide maintaining dignity: now we realise she is in a strop! The waltz metre returns for the final 'A' phrase, and a confident perfect cadence that – finally – conclusively finds the tonic chord.[42]

The scoring of the song is for a dance band: trumpets and saxes to the fore, and some rich bass clarinet on the bass line. There is a very telling short trumpet solo in the opening section at 'one night in his apartment' which calls for the wah-wah mute that gives a suggestive tone.[43]

After Adelaide has sung the refrain, her 'dolls' repeat it in an upbeat $\frac{4}{4}$ version that makes the mood more defiant. A further version for dancing is played as an instrumental.[44]

Here is an annotated version of the essay on British popular music on pages 53–54 of the revision guide.

Choose two songs written in the 1970s, and write in detail about the musical content of each song.

I am going to write about two great songs from the 70s: 'Speak To Me – Breathe' from Pink Floyd's iconic album *The Dark Side of the Moon*, and 'Somebody To Love' by the famous rock band Queen.[45]

Pink Floyd were a London-based band who came to fame in the late 60s with their elaborate light shows. When the line-up changed in 1968, their music changed direction, and became focused on various forms of alienation such as madness and death, which appealed to those growing up in the shadow of Vietnam and the Cold War. *The Dark Side of the Moon* was released in 1973 and is the fifth highest-selling album of all time. 'Speak To Me – Breathe' is the first song on the album.[46]

'Speak To Me' is largely not traditional music but a collage of sound effects starting with a heartbeat, created through a dampened bass drum.[47] Other

41 This time the form of the song is clearly stated.
42 Excellent description of the refrain; do you think the candidate learned all this, or did they have the music running through their mind when writing the essay?
43 This paragraph shows the candidate has **listened** to the music attentively – noting significant aspects of the orchestration – and not just relied on the vocal score.
44 This final paragraph is almost superfluous, since the song turns into a chorus and then a dance number, but it succinctly shows that the rest of the song is known.
45 Candidates are often tempted to spend time writing about what they are going to write about, but it is just a waste of precious time in the exam room and will not gain any marks. Much better just to start writing about the music.
46 Unfortunately, interesting though this paragraph may be, this does not address any musical points. This is a music AS exam: write about music!
47 Good detail about timbre and its intended effect.

sounds heard include ticking clocks, manic laughter, a cash register and a helicopter, all sounds which were to reappear in other songs in the album.[48] There are also fragments of conversation about madness layered on top. At the end a reversed piano chord[49] completes the sense of build-up as the track leads immediately on into 'Breathe'.

'Breathe' has a more clearly defined beat at a slow tempo (typical of Pink Floyd) in four-time. The bass drum gives a strong downbeat to the rhythm.[50] There is a more distinct verse structure here: eight lines that come in two halves – a change of chord sequence marking the halfway point.[51] The same music provides an instrumental introduction with guitars and frequent slow pitch-bending.[52] The song links into the next track on the album, 'On The Run'.

As prosperity grew in the 1970s, pop concerts increasingly were held at large stadiums such as Wembley. The song by Queen 'Somebody To Love' is representative of a style that suits such events, a style now called 'stadium rock'.[53] The song is influenced by gospel music, especially of the style sung by Aretha Franklin.[54] Using the latest in 1970s technology, the band members multi-tracked their voices to create the aural illusion of a 100-strong gospel choir.[55]

The introduction to the song is sung with discreet piano backing and has a free approach to rhythm, with frequent pauses, that is typical of gospel music.[56] The voices start on A♭ and fan out in contrary motion in a homophonic choral style.[57]

When the first verse starts the music goes into a strict tempo (a compound four in a bar) and there is a confident, marching quality, heightened by the harmony that concentrates on major chords and keeps moving towards the sharper dominant key.[58] This is achieved by using a B♭ major chord when the song is in A♭ major.[59] Freddie Mercury sings the melody whilst other members of the band provide the backing vocals in a multi-tracked gospel style. The main melody tends to have a

---

48 Shows awareness of context in terms of the album.
49 The reversed piano chord and layering of conversation fragments is good detail, but rather glosses over the significance of the potential for these aspects in 1970s technology.
50 Some good musical details concerning metre and timbre up to this point in this paragraph.
51 There are fewer details here about structure and harmony; information about the chord patterns would be valuable here – in terms of marks.
52 Good use of technical vocabulary here, but the use of synthesisers has been overlooked, which is, surely, a significant factor for 1970s music.
53 There is less biographical flannel here: we start with a significant factor about the way the decade influenced pop music and this song in particular.
54 Good context of style here; it would be helpful to mention an Aretha Franklin song that shows the connection clearly.
55 This sentence shows good awareness of musical idiom and relevant technology of the decade.
56 Good detail here that supports the assertion of the gospel influence.
57 Good use of technical vocabulary regarding the texture here. Do you think the candidate has learned this, or did they have the music running through their mind when writing the essay?
58 Confident analysis of the elements of rhythm and harmony, with good vocabulary and awareness of the resulting emotional affect.
59 Good technical support of the assertion in the previous sentence.

rising contour that allows for some impassioned singing at the top of the male range. Falsetto is also used at times.[60] The 'somebody to love' line provides an infectious melodic hook, and the drumming (by Roger Taylor) makes heavy use of the crash cymbal.[61]

There are two verses, and then a short middle section which provides a balance to the harmony of the verse by visiting the flat side: D♭ major , G♭ major, and G♭ minor. This then passes into an instrumental solo for the lead guitar (played by Brian May), which is based on the chord sequence of the verse. Voices join in at the end and lead into another vocal verse. This, however, breaks off before the refrain, and the line 'need somebody to love' is repeated many times, building from an a cappella start. A final refrain follows.[62]

There is then a coda with several more repetitions of 'find me somebody to love', with rhythmic hand-clapping providing an infectious feature for audience participation: a significant element of stadium rock.[63]

---

60 The candidate has clearly listened carefully to the song and has spotted issues of vocal technique that are audible to the thoughtful listener.
61 Similarly, the candidate has honed in on the playing of the drums and heard this in some detail.
62 This paragraph shows a secure awareness of the structure of the song. It would be possible to present this in table form, which might be something of a time-saver.
63 A neat way to round off this part of the essay.

Glossary

Anacrusis. The note or notes that form an upbeat (or upbeats) to the first downbeat of a phrase.

Antiphony. A technique where two instrumental groups or two choirs alternate in dialogue.

Appoggiatura. An ornamental note that falls on the beat as a dissonance and then resolves by step onto the main note.

Articulation. The manner in which a series of notes are played with regards to their separation or connection – for example, staccato (separated) or legato (connected).

Augmentation. The lengthening of rhythmic values of a previously heard melody (for example in a fugue), or the widening of an interval.

Auxiliary note. A non-harmony note which is a step above (upper auxiliary) or below (lower auxiliary) the harmony note and returns to it.

Binary form. Two-part structure (AB), usually with both sections repeated.

Chord extension. Chords which add additional 3rds to the third and fifth degree of a triad, creating a 7th, 9th, 11th or 13th. You may have encountered some of these in Area of Study 2c.

Chromatic. The use of non-diatonic notes (notes which are not in the current key). Chromatic notes or chromatic passages are often used for expressive purposes.

Circle of 5ths. A series of chords whose roots are each a 5th lower (or a 4th higher) than the previous one. For example, Em–Am–Dm–G–C.

Col legno. A string technique of playing with the wood of the bow.

Compound metre. Time signature in which the beat divides into three: $\frac{6}{8}$, $\frac{9}{8}$, $\frac{12}{8}$.

Con sordino. An instruction to the performer to play with a mute.

Consonant. Intervals or chords which are stable and sound pleasant (for example, unisons, 3rds, 6ths), as opposed to its opposite, dissonant.

Continuo. Short for 'basso continuo', the continuo instruments form the accompaniment in Baroque music. It may include instruments such as the harpsichord (capable of playing full harmony) and a cello or bassoon reinforcing the bass line.

Contrary motion. Movement of two parts in opposite directions to each other.

Counter-melody. An independent melody which complements a more prominent theme.

Da capo aria. Common aria form of Baroque opera and sacred music. ABA shape, with Da Capo instruction at the end of the B section. The singer may add ornamentation during the repeat.

Diatonic. Using notes that belong to the current key.

Diminished 7th. A four-note chord made up of a diminished triad plus a diminished 7th above the root. Diminished 7ths usually function as dominants of the following chord, with the root of the chord omitted in favour of the minor 9th.

Dominant 7th. A four-note chord built on the dominant (5th) note of the scale. It includes the dominant triad plus a minor 7th above the root.

Double stopping. A string technique of playing more than one string at a time. Also triple and quadruple stopping.

False relation. A chromatic contradiction between two notes sounded simultaneously and in different parts. For example a G natural against a G sharp.

Falsetto. This involves the singing of notes above the normal range of the human voice, normally by male singers.

Glissando. A slide between two notes.

Ground bass. Repeating bass, usually four or eight bars in length, with changing music in the other parts. Popular in Baroque music.

Harmonic. Sometimes known as flageolet note, a technique of lightly touching the string (e.g. on a violin) to produce a high, flute-like sound.

Harmonic rhythm. The rate at which harmony changes in a piece.

Hemiola. The articulation of two units of triple time (*strong-weak-weak*, *strong-weak-weak*) as three units of duple time (*strong-weak*, *strong-weak*, *strong-weak*).

Heterophonic. A texture in which different versions of the same melody are heard simultaneously.

Homophonic. A texture in which one part has a melody and the other parts accompany. In contrast to a polyphonic texture, in which each part has independent melodic interest.

Imitation. A contrapuntal device in which a distinct melodic idea in one part is immediately copied by another part, often at a different pitch, while the first part continues with other music. The imitation is not always strict, but the basic melodic and rhythmic outline should be heard.

Leger line. Additional lines used above or beneath the stave to represent notes that fall outside of its range.

Mediant. The third degree of a major or minor scale.

Melisma. A technique in vocal music, where a single syllable is set over a number of notes in the melody. Such a passage may be described as 'melismatic'.

Middle-eight. A passage that may be used in popular music forms, describing a section (usually consisting of eight bars and containing different music) that prepares the return of the main section.

Mode. Seven-note scales that can be created using only the white notes of a piano keyboard. The dorian can be played beginning on D (i.e. D–E–F–G–A–B–C–D), the mixolydian on G, the aeolian on A and the ionian on C. These interval patterns can then be transposed to any other note. For example, dorian beginning on G (or G dorian) would be G–A–B–C–D–E–F–G.

The modes used in 16th-century church music came to interest later composers looking for an alternative to the major-minor tonal system and have been explored in recent times by various classical, jazz and popular musicians.

Modulation. The process of changing key.

Monophonic. A musical texture that uses a single melodic line.

Multi-track recording. A method of recording (normally for popular music) that allows sound sources to be recorded separately and later combined.

Obbligato. Used in Baroque music to denote an instrumental solo part which must be included.

Overdubbing. A recording technique where an additional musical part is recorded to a previously recorded track. This technique is often used by pop musicians to create additional sounds and add more instruments to an existing recording.

Pedal note. A sustained or continuously repeated pitch, often in the bass, that is heard against changing harmonies. A pedal on the fifth degree of the scale (known as the dominant pedal) tends to generate excitement, while a pedal on the key note (known as the tonic pedal) tends to create a feeling of repose.

Phrasing. In performance the execution of longer groups of notes which follow natural patterns of the music. 'Articulation' may be used to refer to phrasing over a shorter group of notes. Phrases may be indicated by the composer but the skill and judgement of the performer is also important in creating a successful performance.

Polyphonic. A texture consisting of two or more equally important melodic lines heard together. In contrast to a homophonic texture, in which one part has the melody and the other parts accompany. The term polyphonic has a similar meaning to contrapuntal, but is more often used for vocal rather than instrumental music.

Portamento. A slide between two notes.

Power chord. A term used in popular music to refer to a chord for guitar that omits the 3rd of the triad. It therefore contains a bare interval of a 5th.

Recitative. A technique in opera and oratorio where the singer conveys the text in a speech-like manner. This is normally used to cover narrative effectively and contrasts with arias which are much more lyrical.

Ritornello. In Baroque music, the repeated tutti section used as a refrain; most often in the first or last movement of a concerto, or in arias or choral works.

Rubato. The alteration of rhythm, particularly in a melodic line, by lengthening and shortening notes but keeping an overall consistent tempo.

Scotch snap. A two-note dotted rhythm which has the shorter note on the beat. Usually an on-beat semiquaver followed by an off-beat dotted quaver. Also known as lombardic rhythm.

Segue. The continuation of one section or movement to another without a break. In popular albums, this refers to one track immediately following its predecessor.

Sequence. Immediate repetition of a melodic or harmonic idea at a different pitch, or a succession of different pitches.

Sonata form. Typical first movement form of the Classical and Romantic periods. In three sections – exposition, development, recapitulation – often based on two groups of melodic material in two contrasting keys (first subject, second subject).

Strophic. A song in which the music is repeated for each verse, for example a hymn.

Sul ponticello. A string technique of playing close to the bridge.

Syncopation. Placing the accents in parts of the bar that are not normally emphasised, such as on weak beats or between beats, rather than in the expected place on strong beats.

Tessitura. A specific part of a singer's or instrument's range. For example a 'high tessitura' indicates a high part of the range.

Through-composed. A stage work (opera or musical) in which the music is not split into seperate numbers. Also a song in which there is different music composed for each verse.

Tierce de Picardie. A major 3rd in the final tonic chord of a passage in a minor mode.

Tritone. An interval that is equivalent to three tones (an augmented 4th or dimished 5th).

Voicing. The arrangement of pitches within a chord to create a particular texture.

Word painting. A technique of setting text in which the sound or movement implied by a word or phrase is imitated by the music (e.g. a falling phrase for 'dying').